What Readers Are Saying About

Agile and Lean Program Management: Scaling Collaboration Across the Organization

"This is the book for everyone who is considering how to "scale" their lean/agile processes to work in large programs. Johanna provides straightforward and practical advice on how to go from single project/simple product agile implementation to large, complex programs while retaining the core of agility and lean thinking. She takes us back to the fundamental principles of agile and lean and shows how to use those principles as a foundation for true organisational agility, building products that need multiple teams with different interdependent streams of work while retaining the adaptability and responsiveness that is at the core of lean and agile thinking."

—SHANE HASTIE, CHIEF KNOWLEDGE ENGINEER & AGILE PRACTICE LEAD, SOFTWARE EDUCATION

"Johanna Rothman's new book is the definitive guide to programme management in the agile and lean world. I found it invaluable in crystallising in my mind how to marry agile and lean principles to programme management. It's a book that you will turn to when somebody asks you a tricky question that you know will be better articulated by Johanna."

—OWAIN GRIFFITHS, PRINCIPAL CONSULTANT, THOUGHTWORKS

"In *Agile and Lean Program Management*, Johanna does a wonderful job of blending tried and true concepts for modern software program delivery with newer models and ideas. And, as always, she does a great job providing practical, pragmatic approaches to using the ideas she provides. A must-read for anyone who is either responsible for or impacted by the planning or delivery of multi-team software initiatives."

—MATT BARCOMB, DIRECTING PRINCIPAL, TIDAL RIVER CONSULTING

"Johanna has created an excellent guide to managing large (aka enterprise) projects. By taking the large, often unwieldy, concepts and placing them in an experienced agile/lean context, she makes the information accessible and provides the roadmap you need to keep your organization on track and effective."

—JARED RICHARDSON, PRINCIPAL CONSULTANT, AGILE ARTISANS

"How do you scale Agile software practices (best suited for single teams of 5-10 developers) to larger programmes spanning multiple disciplines and multiple teams? This is the most useful description I have seen: Johanna shows how you can apply the principles of Lean and Agile software development with actionable, pragmatic techniques to deliver the value your customers desire."

—IAN BROCKBANK, AGILE ARCHITECT AND PROGRAM MANAGER, CIRRUS LOGIC, AND BLOGGER AT WWW.BADGERTAMING.NET

"*Agile and Lean Program Management* provides the practical and principled advice to make your large product efforts a success. Johanna wisely avoids the confusion and misdirection of contemporary conversations around "scaling agile." She also avoids hierarchies, strict role definitions, and building a giant process machine. This allows Agile and Lean Program Management to focus on what's really important for any large product effort: effective communication, clear expectations, customer focus, collaboration, and acting from principles. Johanna strikes an excellent balance between the practical and the theoretical here—and achieves a conversational tone even when diving into the latter. This book feels like sitting down with a trusted colleague to chat and get some guidance on ideas, patterns, and solutions."

—GARY PEDRETTI, AGILE TRAINER AND OWNER, SODOTO SOLUTIONS

AGILE and LEAN
Program Management

Scaling Collaboration
Across the Organization

Johanna Rothman

Agile and Lean Program Management

Scaling Collaboration Across the Organization

Johanna Rothman

Published by Practical Ink

www.jrothman.com

Practical **ink**

Cover art: © Csuzda | Dreamstime.com—Team Growth Photo
Cover: Lucky Bat Books

Print: 978-1-943487-07-3
PDF: 978-1-943487-04-2
Epub: ISBN: 978-1-943487-05-9
Mobi: 978-1-943487-06-6

For my family.
Thank you for your support.

Contents

CHAPTER 1

CHAPTER 2

CHAPTER 6

Create an Environment of Delivery 67

CHAPTER 7

Encourage Autonomy, Collaboration, and Exploration . . 77

List of Figures

Acknowledgments

I thank my Managing Product Development[1] blog readers. Your comments made my ideas better. I thank these people who read and reviewed the book and provided me feedback: Matt Barcomb, Arlo Belshee, Ian Brockbank, Clarke Ching, George Dinwiddie, Paul Ellarby, Lior Friedman, Owain Griffiths, Matt Heusser, Gary Pedretti, Catherine Swetel, Michael Vizdos, Rebecca Wirfs-Brock.

I thank my editors, Rebecca Airmet and Nancy Groth. I thank Karen Billipp for the layout and Jean Jesensky for indexing the print book.

Cover art: © Csuzda | Dreamstime.com—Team Growth Photo
Cover: Lucky Bat Books.

---

[1] http://www.jrohtman.com/blog/mpd

Foreword

I wish this book had been published the last time I ran a major project; it is a pragmatic and action based, but in a way that is also consistent with theory—something that is all too rare. The Agile community, as a whole, is riddled with rigid methods imposed with religious zeal to support training and certification programs. In contrast this book understands that scaling Agile is about the assembly of different tools, methods, and practices to achieve a result within a specific context. It has a whole section on what to do when Agile is not a cultural match for the organization. While it is predicated on servant leadership, it recognizes that this does not "mean you are a pushover." Sometimes you have to remove team members.

The early chapters do not mandate a process, and there are few of the engineering-type diagrams that overprescribe and overstructure what should be seen as a service delivery. Instead, they ask a series of questions with a range of suggested responses depending upon the answer. This is not a *one-size-fits-all* handbook, but a *many-things-might-work, think-before-you-act* assembly approach. Critically, it does not run away from the idea that management is necessary. One of the early phrases I highlighted was: "Some people call program management scaling agile. You could call it that. The real name is program management." Managing a program is a mixture of strategic and tactical needs, and the two need to co-exist and interact to create resilient and adaptive solutions. By combining Lean and Agile with a basic understanding of complexity (it uses my Cynefin framework), the book sets out a roadmap by which a program can be a unique assembly of appropriate methods and tools derived from multiple sources.

As the world requires shorter cycle delivery against increasingly poorly articulated needs, we need more of this deeply pragmatic thinking. Scaling is not about grand frameworks geared to making people comfortable and securing training revenues. It is about sound advice, good questions, and adaptive and flexible management. This book is a great contribution addressing that need and I am grateful for the opportunity to write this Foreword.

—Professor Dave Snowden,
Chief Scientific Officer, Cognitive Edge

Introduction

We hear a lot of buzz about "scaling agile."

Instead of "scaling agile," consider "scale projects to a program." Program management is how we move from coordinating one project's work to coordinating the work of several projects in a program. When your product requires you to collaborate across the organization, you need agile and lean program management.

Program management is not a new idea. What might be new for you is the application of servant leadership to the program manager role. If you want to use agile and lean approaches, you, as a program manager, serve the program. You trust people to do the right thing, and manage by exception.

You use program management anytime you want to scale collaborative teams across the organization. Here are some possibilities:

- You are a project manager, trying to corral a few teams together, to release a product.
- You are a manager who needs several teams to collaborate on one strategic objective.
- You need to have the hardware and software people work together to release a product.
- You need Marketing or Sales or Training or some other function(s) to work with the software people to release a product.

You might have a difference circumstance for your program. All programs have one thing in common—the people collaborate across the organization to deliver the product. Whatever your product is, you or your team alone can't ensure that your product releases, no matter how agile or lean you are, when your team says, "Done!"

Programs are strategic collections of projects with one business objective. Program managers coordinate that one business objective across the organization.

When you coordinate across the organization, you recognize the need for the other teams—regardless of their function—to maintain their autonomy in how they create their deliverables. For programs, everyone comes together to serve the program's needs. Everyone optimizes for the program, not for their team.

Each program is unique. Some of you will have software-only programs. Some of you will want to use this book for products that include software, hardware, firmware, and mechanical components. That's why this book is based on principles, not mandates.

Principle-based agile and lean might also be new for you, too. Remember, that if you duplicate what works in small projects to larger programs, all you get is bloat. Bloat doesn't deliver—at least, not easily. Take the principles of agile and lean, and think, "How can I apply these principles to my context?"

Whether you are a team member on a feature team, a core team member, or the program manager, this book has something for you. Why? Because the agile and lean program is a complex adaptive system. Everyone has his or her own role to play. And, everyone in the agile and lean program has to be aware of the entire rest of the program. No one succeeds without everyone else succeeding.

This book will help you see how to use agile and lean approaches to manage your program. Here's to your success. Now, let's start.

CHAPTER 1

Defining Agile and Lean Program Management

Imagine this scenario:

You're the program manager for an entire product. You arrive at work and check your email. You discover that one of the feature teams found a Big Hairy problem, but they fixed it with the help of another team. Did you need to intervene? No. Neither did the software program manager. Yes, your program is large enough—18 feature teams—that you need a software program manager also.

You're meeting with the core team today. Ellie, the Marketing Communications rep to the core team has been working on her deliverables for a couple of weeks. The feature teams know they have to provide performance information so Mar-Comm can finish their glossies. MarComm knows their deliverables are key to a successful product launch.

Once you explained how to set up a kanban in MarComm, they all got "kanban fever." Well, it seems that way. They love watching those stickies move across the board. The core team understands how their deliverables intersect with everyone else's deliverables now, and why it's so critical that their parts are complete and done when they commit to dates. Everyone on the core team is talking about "done." "We sound just like the software teams," they say.

The program architect was concerned about the architecture evolution just two months ago. He'd never seen an architecture evolve. He'd always planned the architecture in advance. Then the architecture evolved anyway. You and the program product owner and the software program manager all felt as if you talked him "off the cliff." He conceded, and was willing to try to evolve the architecture.

Surprisingly enough, the product is simpler than he thought—right now. He's coding, for the first time in years. He's happy. So are the feature teams. They feel as if they are part of the design thinking, not just taking orders from some guy with his head in the clouds.

Senior management is happy with you, because every month you demonstrate something real, even if it's small. It's only been three months and you have a release candidate. R&D has never been able to produce something that fast. Three months into the program and you have a working product that the company can sell. Well, once MarComm finishes their deliverables.

Is this a fantasy? No. This is how agile and lean program management works. In fact, with the exception of the kanban board, that is how I worked in 1988 on a real product, in a real organization. Many successful programs repeat these principles: build trust among the teams on the program; deliver often to see feedback; build trust across the organization.

Let's review the agile and lean principles so you can consider how to apply them to your program.

1.1 Review the Twelve Principles of Agile Software Development

The list below paraphrases the twelve primary principles of agile software development. See the source for the original principles at the Agile Manifesto Principles.[1]

---

[1] http://www.agilemanifesto.org/principles.html

1. Deliver early and often to satisfy the customer.
2. Welcome changing requirements.
3. Deliver working software frequently.
4. Business people and developers must work together.
5. Trust motivated people to do their jobs.
6. Face-to-face conversation is the most efficient and effective method of conveying information.
7. Working software is the primary measure of progress.
8. Maintain a sustainable pace.
9. Continuous attention to technical excellence and good design enhances agility.
10. Simplicity—the art of maximizing the amount of work not done—is essential.
11. The best architectures, requirements, and designs emerge from self-organizing teams.
12. Reflect and adjust at regular intervals.

The point of the agile principles is that you collaborate across the organization, seeing working product as a way to work with the customer and make sure you are on track. You work in a way that enhances technical excellence so you can accommodate change. You inspect and adapt as you proceed, on the product and the process, so that you can fine-tune your team and product.

1.2 Review the Seven Lean Principles

In *Lean Software Development: An Agile Toolkit*, POP03, Mary and Tom Poppendieck summarized their lean approach with these seven principles.

1. Eliminate waste.
2. Amplify learning.
3. Decide as late as possible.
4. Deliver as fast as possible.
5. Empower the team.

6. Build integrity in.
7. See the whole.

Lean principles help you see the whole process (for a team or a program or anything in-between). You consider when to make decisions and learn as you proceed. Lean encourages you to see the entire product.

Use the agile and lean principles as you manage risk and solve problems in the program. Consider how you can apply them to your program.

The principles help you understand how to use agile and lean on your program.

1.3 Agile and Lean Together Create Adaptive Programs

When you use agile and lean principles, you can create and steer an adaptive, resilient program. When I use the word, "program," from now on, please think "agile and lean" or "adaptive."

1.4 A Program Is a Strategic Collection of Several Projects

A program is a collection of projects, where the value is in the overall deliverable. Yes, each project may have a deliverable that's valuable. However, the value to the organization is when all the projects get together and deliver their product. That is a concurrent program. You may also have a serial program, such as delivering a series of releases over a product's lifetime.

Think of a smartphone as an example of a strategic collection of several projects. One project might be the feature set that allows the phone to make and answer a call. Another project could be the feature set to access and leave voicemail. Another two feature sets might be the accounting for the voice data and the download data. The texting feature set would be another project. Do you see how each set of features could be its own project?

Each of these projects might require one or more feature teams working together. The teams work autonomously, however they like, as long as they are agile or lean, delivering their completed features often. Each project and team works in parallel. Each project has its own rhythm and staff and backlog. The projects deliver a working product as a program.

Beware of a collection of ranked backlogs with no strategic reason behind the order. If there isn't a larger business objective behind the backlogs, it's not a program. You might need to accomplish all that work. And, if the ranked backlogs together don't create a coherent business value, where the entire product is more valuable than each project, you don't have a program.

Can you have waterfall teams with your agile and lean teams and still have a successful program? It depends on whether the waterfall teams have interdependencies with the agile and lean teams. Make sure you read Integrating Agile and Not-Agile Teams in Your Program (page 195).

Each program needs a coherent vision behind the program so you can create a program charter. The charter helps the feature teams take responsibility for their tradeoffs. We'll talk more about this in Start Your Program Right (page 35). With a program charter in place, the feature teams won't need to work up and then down a hierarchy.

Some people call program management "scaling agile." You could call it that. The real name is program management. In program management, you scale agile and lean collaboration practices across the entire program, so you can release a great product.

1.5 Program Management Facilitates the Program to Release

Program management is the coordination and facilitation of all of the work across the organization to release the product.

The job of the program manager is to coordinate the teams so they understand enough about each other's risks so they *can* deliver. The program manager does not and cannot do this alone. The program is all about collaboration.

 Projects are tactical; they get the work done. The program is strategic. It ties the projects together to bring them to delivery.

1.6 Program Management Coordinates the Business Value

I've seen—and I bet you have too—programs where the software was all done except for one small piece. The product couldn't release because that piece was vital to the release. Or the software was done but the marketing was not. Or the hardware was done, the marketing was done, and the software was stuck.

If you employ agile approaches to programs, you get to see visible progress (or lack thereof) at the end of each iteration or the end of each feature in flow or as the teams create the product. You don't have to wait until the predicted or desired end of the program to see the risk.

That's one of the ways agile reduces technical and schedule risk. The iterations or flow help you get to done across the entire program. Each iteration helps you see how things fit together. The demonstration at the end of an iteration (or at a milestone) shows you where you have technical risk, which reduces schedule risk. In general, incremental approaches reduce schedule risk and iterative approaches reduce technical risk. Because agile combines both, you reduce both kinds of risk. For more detail on life cycles, see *Manage It! Your Guide to Modern, Pragmatic Project Management*, (ROT07).

If you use lean approaches to your program, you can reduce the work in progress, which will allow you to maximize throughput. A lean approach will enable you to see bottlenecks, reduce waste, and see what is not getting done. You need both agile and lean for a program.

You don't have to release each iteration or feature to your customers. You can decide when to release externally—that's a business decision. When you see completed work each feature or each iteration is how you know you provide business value.

1.7 Agile Program Management Scales Collaboration

In non-agile program management, project managers or functional managers speak for their project teams or functional area. They commit people, manage risks, and commit other resources, such as money. Notice that there is no program-specific view of the product or transparent coordination across the functional teams. Those programs may not have a ranked product backlog.

In program management, there is no hierarchy. Everyone collaborates and coordinates across the cross-functional teams. This collaboration avoids Coordination Chaos as in TIK14.

The program teams solve problems cross-functionally. That's a huge difference.

Instead of functional managers committing on behalf of functional teams, feature teams commit to the program. The program team has the responsibility for removing obstacles so that the program delivers the business value of the program.

Lean thinking adds the holistic view to the program. When we add lean, we empower teams and eliminate waste. We amplify everyone's learning to build integrity into the product by seeing the work in progress, sharing decisions, and having a fine-grained definition of done. This is critical, because the more people we have, the more chances we have to learn and to make mistakes. If we take a lean approach at the beginning, we start with principles that make sense for building great products.

In the same way that good project management was never about command-and-control, good program management is not command-and-control. Good program management is servant leadership.

Program management enables coordination: helping the teams and projects to collaborate to deliver some specific business objectives.

Once your program has more than two teams, or you need to coordinate with multiple people across the organization, releasing your product becomes much more difficult. Program management helps you coordinate across the organization, so that everyone focuses on the goal: releasing a great product that works.

1.8 Agile and Lean Effect Change at the Program Level

Agile is about the ability to change by delivering running, tested features that are valuable to the business and learning from that work. Lean is about seeing the whole, the flow of your work, building integrity into your work, and eliminating waste. If you add the technical practices (which you must in a large program), the program makes visible the values of simplicity, respect, and courage. Everyone commits to their work. You create empowered teams.

You will get increased speed as a byproduct if you have the ability to change. You will get speed if you reduce your work in progress (WIP) and waste.

No management can mandate agile and lean at the program level. Feature teams who can adapt and work together with a product focus create the agile and lean program.

As a result of transitioning to agile and lean in the teams, and using adaptive program management, you will obtain better delivery-to-market speed as a result.

1.9 What Program Managers Do

The program manager is the voice or the face of the program. The program manager represents the program to the PMO (Project Management Office) or to senior managers in the organization. As a program manager, I reported to the Operations Committee, a team of senior managers.

The program manager facilitates the collaboration across the organization. The program manager is a servant leader. Program management doesn't drive anything to completion; program managers enable the program participants to finish their work.

1.10 Take a Product Perspective

You may have noticed I have been talking about your "product." You might have applications that you refer to as "systems." You might integrate several systems from other vendors. Some of you might have something else.

I take a product-centric view of things. I suggest you do, too. If you think all the time, "Who is the customer for this?" you might have some insights about how to use agile and lean to deliver.

"I Think 'Product' Now"

I used to think about systems or applications. I've been a program manager doing in-house financial applications for years.

When I started to think about "products" instead of "applications" a funny thing happened. Other people started talking about product, too. The product owners on the program started to talk about their customers differently. They started to name their users, with specific personas. I did not expect that to happen.

Our stories got smaller. Our feature teams produced more value, because they got to done on smaller stories faster. All because I started talking about "product," not "application."

—*An experienced program manager*

Okay. Now you know what an agile or lean program is. Let's talk about how you might organize your program.

1.11 Principles of Agile and Lean Program Management

1. Take a product perspective. The principle is: "Business people and developers must work together."

2. Agile and lean approaches encourage a holistic approach to the product where you can change more easily to meet current needs. The principle is: "Welcome changing requirements. This is a competitive advantage."

3. Program managers are servant leaders. The principles are: "Build projects around motivated individuals," "Trust them to get the job done," and "Empower the team."

CHAPTER 2

Consider Your Program Context

You and all the members of your program will make multiple decisions on a daily basis. The Cynefin Framework is a way of thinking about your context with the intent of guiding your actions. I use Cynefin to think about how I solve problems: Can we use good practices that everyone else uses? Do we need to experiment to know how to proceed? Do we have so many unknowns that we don't know where to start?

2.1 Cynefin Helps with Decisions

The Cynefin Framework (SNB07) is a sense-making framework you can use to solve problems. Use it to guide your approach to your program. See Figure 2.1 on page 12.

Based on the fact you are working in a program, you are not in the Obvious context. A program, by its very nature, is at least in the Complicated context, because of the number of communication paths.

If everyone is in a single physical location, you may be in the Complicated context. In the Complicated context, you can see straight cause-and-effect relationships among the different stresses in your program. If all your teams are experienced agile or lean teams, who know how to deliver small stories each day or so, you might be in the Complicated context. You understand what your unknowns are. You can use known and reasonable practices for organizing and working on your agile program.

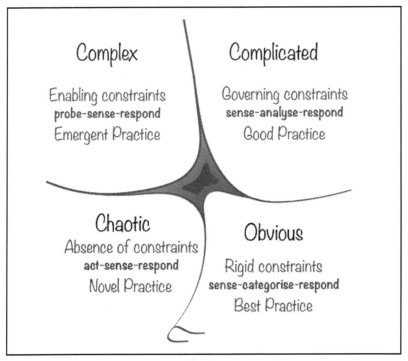

Figure 2.1: Cynefin Framework

As soon as you and the people in your program are not in the same location, you are no longer in the Complicated context. You have moved into either the Complex or Chaotic context. That's because your communication will have delivery or communication lags and other interferences. Problem causes or effects may be unclear and even unknown, if only due to communication lags.

If people on your program are multitasking, or if you have people or teams who can't commit to the program, or if many of your feature teams are new to agile, you are at least in the Complex context. You may be in the Chaotic context. In either of these contexts, the unknowns create many risks and potential problems.

In my experience, if you can say, "We have done work like this, but never at this complexity or with this many teams, or never as distributed as we are now," you are in the Complex context. You have many unknown unknowns. You will have to manage the risk of those unknowns.

As you look at the Cynefin Framework, ask yourself: what context reflects your reality? How will that context help you decide whether you should sense, probe, or act as an experiment first?

If you are in the Complicated part of the framework, you need experts to solve the problems in your program. I'm not talking about experts that create bottlenecks by working alone. Instead, develop a community of experts—maybe most of the people on your program, working in their Communities of Practice—to help solve the problems.

If you are in the Complex part of the framework, consider these actions: What experiments will you use to probe, to discover your unknowns? And, what problems can you solve to move the program back to the Complicated part of the framework, where you can know your challenges?

Cynefin is not a two-by-two matrix where you locate your program, use that to make decisions, and never return to the framework. Instead, especially with programs of nine teams or more, different parts of the program will have different challenges. The more unknowable the challenges, the more that part of the program is in the Complex part of the framework. As the teams deliver features, they learn more. That part of the program moves to the Complicated part of the framework.

Sometimes, teams in the Complicated part of the framework finish features. As they learn, they uncover a huge "gotcha." That might cause them to be in the Complex part of the framework until they run some experiments to see what they can do.

As a program manager, how can you identify issues early when you encounter Complex again? How can you help the program move from Complex to Complicated?

There are no easy answers. There is no recipe. This is work. It's the reason why we need program management, to recognize and solve problems across the organization.

The Cynefin Framework reveals why agile program management can be difficult. As teams complete their features, the product owners need to update the roadmap and the backlogs. It's possible the program will finish before expected. Completing—or not—other projects or programs may affect the organization's project portfolio. Certainly, one team's feature completion might affect the ability of other teams to deliver.

Regardless of your context, a program is emergent. With emergent projects, you can't plan everything at the beginning. You can see a roadmap, plan a little, and continue learning and adapting as you proceed. You might want to keep the same vision of the product, but teams (with their product owners) might select different work. Or, as your customers/product owners see the product, they might want to change the product direction.

If the teams don't complete features on a short, regular basis, no one can understand what the program status is. If the core team doesn't solve problems that allow the program to create a *product*, you have plenty of risks, many of them unknown.

 Manage by principles, not practices.

With your risks, consider principles for your program, not practices. I could try to create a recipe for you, but that won't work. Think and recognize your context.

2.2 Understand Your Product's Complexity

Your program is unique. Your program may have complexity in a variety of areas: architecture, pressure to release, where the people sit in relationship to each other, the languages everyone uses, and each team's agility.

In my experience, the overall architecture of your product can drive much of the complexity. The more complex the architecture and the larger your program is, the more complexity you will have to manage. Here are some program architectures I have seen.

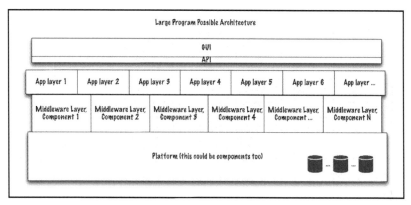

Figure 2.2: Large Program, One Coherent Product

In this case, you have one large product. It's not integrating other products or systems. Your program creates the entire product. It's big with multiple feature teams, which is why you have complexity in your program.

As an example, an operating system might look like one coherent product. Maybe a large web-based store might look like one coherent product.

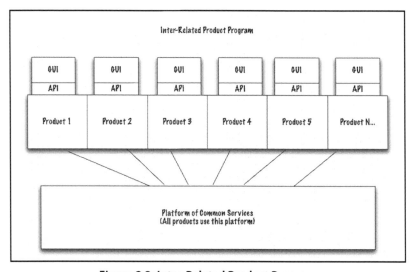

Figure 2.3: Inter-Related Product Program

Inter-related products are different. If you ever say, "Platform and layered products," you have an example of an inter-related product.

In this case, you have a platform of common services with what feel to the customer as separate products. The GUIs may have their own look and feel, but the GUI is not common across your program's product.

As an example, a smartphone is an integrated system product. Each app on the phone has its own GUI where you set the preferences and use the app. Each app uses services from the phone's operating system.

Sometimes, inter-related products integrate other products into the one product.

It's more likely if you integrate other vendors' products into your own, that you have an integrated system program.

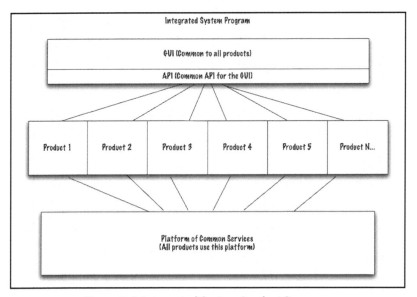

Figure 2.4: Integrated System Product Program

In this case, customers buy your entire product. The product still has the platform of common services. However, you have one coherent

GUI that the products have to integrate with. You might be integrating systems or hardware from vendors.

These programs tend to need programs of programs. Different products will run on their own schedule. Unless your vendors are also agile and lean, you may have to manage integration risks.

2.3 Know Which Program Teams You Need

Every program needs the ability to work across the organization. You might need a *core team*, the cross-functional business team that has members from all around the organization. The core team helps coordinate the efforts that make the entire product a successful deliverable.

If you have more than two feature teams, you might also need a *software program team*. The software program team helps deliver the working software. The software program manager is a delegate to the core program team. That means that the software program manager must have a program team of his/her own. This is true for a large program.

You, as a program manager, need to understand which program teams you need. Does your program require both a core team and a software program team? Do you need a core team program manager and a software program team manager?

You can only manage one program team. One of the problems I see in too many agile programs is that they have neither a core team nor a software program team. They have many feature or component teams. They might have Scrum-of-Scrum meetings, but no real forum for solving the deep problems or managing the risks that can occur across the organization.

Each program team has a responsibility to solve problems that the teams it represents can't solve by themselves. The program team, whether it is a core team or a software program team, works across the organization, solving problems and removing obstacles for the program.

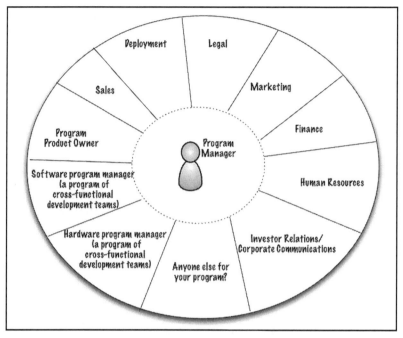

Figure 2.5: What Your Core Team Might Look Like

If you are coordinating and collaborating across the entire organization, you are managing or are a part of the *core* team. If you take a look at the What Your Core Team Might Look Like, you can see that there are plenty of potential participants on this program team.

Do You Have A Process Program?

Sometimes, organizations run process improvement projects, such as transitioning to agile, as if they are programs. That's fine. In this, your core team will look different. You might not have feature teams in your program.

Know what kind of a program you have. Not all programs are the same. Use a core team that makes sense for your program.

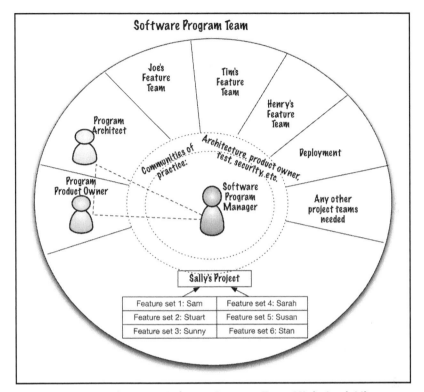

Figure 2.6: What Your Software Program Team Might Look Like

Aside from the program manager, there is the software program manager, the potential hardware program manager, the program product owner, as well as the sales, deployment, legal, marketing, finance, human resources, and investor relations project managers. And those are only the people I could imagine. There might be other or different people in your organization.

Take a look at What Your Software Program Team Might Look Like (above) to see a prototype composition.

Notice that the program product owner and the program architect might work as a triad with the software program manager to make risk decisions. Does this mean that the program product owner does not work with the core program manager?

It depends. It depends on who needs the program product owner. Maybe you need a product owner team, and the program product owner works with the core team and the technical product owner works with the software program owner. It depends on what your program needs.

Look at the program architect. Your feature teams need their own architects on their teams. Sally's project—which is its own program—needs its own architect. That architect better talk to the program architect. And if there's a hardware architect, that architect better talk to the program architect. So you might need a cross-functional community of practice architecture team, as illustrated in the "communities of practice" architecture team.

If you are a program manager, first, are you on the core team? If so, do you have everyone you need? Does that team have responsibility for deployment? (I don't care who has responsibility for deployment, as long as someone does.)

If you are not on the core team, are you on the technical team that works across the technology? Does this team have responsibility for deployment? I'm being a little touchy about deployment because I have consulted to programs where no one was responsible for deployment and they only discovered it when I asked, "Who's responsible for deployment?" I thought I was being stupid because I didn't see it. No, no one had thought about it. Oops.

Why do you need all these program teams? The core team might require a different rhythm than the software program team. Since the core team often has senior managers or senior people on it, I recommend the core team use kanban to reduce the WIP (work in progress). The software program teams can use iterations if that works for them. Maybe they also use kanban; it doesn't matter. The two program teams address different risks at different levels.

The core program team is much more strategic. Often program managers at this level manage budgets and project portfolio issues. They are the ones to say, "Wait a minute. The software program can't succeed. We need to merge these two products." That's a project portfolio issue.

The software program team is more strategic than a given project, but is not as likely to manage budget or a project portfolio issue.

Program management, especially for many teams (think more than 20 teams) is about making sure you have a product that delivers the business value you want from all that effort. So the software program will have its own risks and rhythm, which is separate from the core team's risks and rhythm.

If you are a program manager, make sure you know which team you are trying to manage (coordinate and collaborate), so you can be most effective. Remember, you can only manage one program team. (See Don't Manage More Than One Program Team Yourself, page 32, for more details.)

2.4 The Core Team Provides Business Leadership and Value

The core team sets the agenda and the vision for the program. The core team helps the feature teams when they need it, and stays out of their way when they don't need it. The feature teams provide status to the core team, so that the core team can share status across the organization. The core team can adapt their risk management, including the program roadmap, if necessary.

Your core team delegates are essential to your program's success. Ask yourself—and maybe the people who could be on the core team— these questions:

- Do you have the authority to commit to budget decisions for this program? Can you approve spending?
- Do you have time to commit to this program?
- Are there people or project teams that you can commit to this program?
- Can you commit other people or resources to this program?

- Can you commit to the success of this program?

When the core team members are committed to the program's success, they can solve problems more easily.

Here are the responsibilities of the core team before the program starts:

- Write the program charter.
- Create the agile roadmap.
- Create the program backlog, the backlog of features.

This is what the core team does during the program:

- Iterate on the agile roadmap.
- Iterate on the program backlog, the backlog of features.
- Solve cross-functional business problems.
- Solve problems that escalate from the software program team.
- Monitor product status and risks.
- Clear program obstacles for the teams.
- Decide when the product is ready to release.

The core team does all of this because they are responsible for the business value of the program. Because the core team is cross-functional, the people on the core team can help different departments and projects understand how they are interdependent.

The core team embodies the principle of business people and developers working together.

2.5 Do You Need a Core Team?

You might not need a core team if you have a small program. You might need a software program team with a few cross-functional people, such as the person who shepherds the product to release, maybe called Deployment or Release.

Imagine you have a web-based product. Maybe you only have four or five feature teams. Those feature teams want to know what Marketing and Deployment are also doing—and they want to know what all the software teams are doing, too. In that case, maybe you can keep just one program team and have all the necessary people on that team.

Try to keep the number of people on your program team to ten or fewer. Otherwise, it's difficult to make decisions.

If you have the core team and the software program team as a mixed program team, be aware that you may have trouble solving problems and managing risks. The people on the mixed program team will want to solve problems at different levels, and you'll have too many people on your core team.

2.6 Principles of Consider Your Program Context

1. Consider your complexity. If your organization wants to start a brand new agile program on a highly complex architecture with geographically distributed teams when you have not succeeded with agile at the team level, your risks will be different than if the entire organization has agile experience. The principles are: "Amplify learning" and "See the whole."

2. Define which program teams your program needs. The principle is: "Business people and developers must work together."

3. Consider how you will help your program team deliver what the organization requires. The principle is: "Eliminate waste."

CHAPTER 3

Organize Your Program Teams

Each program is unique. Once you understand your program context, you can decide how to guide your program to success.

3.1 Create Your Core Team

Your core team are your allies across the organization. They are the people who will help you move the product from an idea to a fully completed and shippable product.

You need one person from each *necessary* function across the organization, and not more than one person.

Back in What Your Core Team Might Look Like (page 18), you saw a picture of a possible core team. You might not have a hardware program manager, for example. Maybe you don't need anyone from investor relations to release your product.

No matter what, make sure that you have some form of deployment, either in your core team or in the software program team. It doesn't matter which team that person sits on, as long as you have a deployment person somewhere on a program team.

It doesn't matter what you call the deployment person either: Release Engineering, DevOps, IT, or something else. Make sure you have someone whose responsibility is to make sure your product successfully deploys.

Your core team needs people who can commit their time, and their department's time to solve problems, as well as budget. If you can identify the specific person you need, that's the best. If you only know the role, that's okay. But you also need to know the level of that role in the organization.

Make sure you ask the questions in The Core Team Provides Business Leadership (page 21). That way, you know you have the right people at the right level on the core team.

In the past, I have had problems gathering everyone on my core teams. The sales guy didn't want to commit to a biweekly meeting. He was "too busy." The MarComm woman was too frantic doing other things. The corporate lawyer never answered his email.

I needed those people for a successful product release. Without them, we couldn't know if we had the right dates, if we all understood the risks. We would be up the proverbial creek.

How could I make it worth their while to come to the core team meetings?

I have done these things:

1. Asked a specific person by name. "Mary, can you please work on my new program with me? I enjoyed working with you on that last program. I'd like to do it again." When you ask a person *by name* for help, that person is more likely to say yes. If you put out a request on email, everyone feels free to ignore it.

2. Asked a senior manager to assign "the best person" in his or her department. I've had this conversation with a senior manager more than once: "John, you know that I'm the program manager for the XYZ program, which is the company's #1 priority. I need someone from Training on the core team. I need your best person, not just to represent Training. That person will develop new training materials as Software develops the product, and as Deployment gets ready for release. We will be ready as an organization to release, all on the same day. That's why I need your very best person." I use the Voice of Reason, along with the Steely Eyed Glare and a big smile. I almost always get what I ask for.

3. I use influence, where I think, "What will make it worthwhile for this senior manager to give me what I want?" This is why you need to know why the organization wants to start the program. I have discussed the program's deliverables with an eye to the business benefit for the senior manager.

I always tell the members of the core team that we are the best people in the organization to work on this product—that we can collaborate and shepherd this product to its final release. That's why the organization chose us.

I believe this. Why else would the organization spend money on the program?

3.2 Beware of Forgetting Core Team Members

When I coach program managers, sometimes they discover they have overlooked people or key players for the core team. Sometimes they forget because the program is small and the core team is rolled into the software program team. Sometimes it's because the program manager invites the correct people and they don't respond in a reasonable amount of time. Sometimes, there's a power play at work at a higher level in the organization. Sometimes, it's another reason.

Do you have some commonly "omitted" roles on your programs? Review your core team members. Do you have everyone you need, to release a product?

If not, ask people to participate, or enlist the senior manager in that area to help you find the right person for your core team.

3.3 The Product Owner Role Is Key to the Program's Success

It doesn't matter if we talk about the program product owner or a product owner on a team. Each product owner has a key role to play on a program.

The program product owner, sometimes known as the PPO, or the delegate to the program team, shepherds the business value of the roadmap and of the releases. The PPO represents the product owners to the rest of the program team. The PPO is a servant leadership position. Your organization might call the PPO a product manager.

The product owner, sometimes known as the PO, is the person on the feature team who understands what the customers want and translates that understanding to stories. You may also need a subject matter expert such as an architect or senior technical person to work with the PO. The PO, or the PO team, or the PO and the program architect assess which features to do first, the technical challenges with those features, and the Cost of Delay for each feature.

If you have a highly complex product with many feature teams, consider a product owner value team.

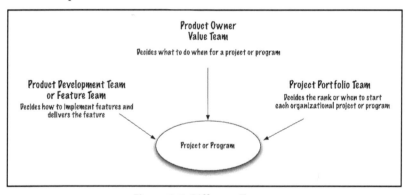

Figure 3.1: Different Teams

In this scenario, the feature team (product development team) implements a feature. The product value team decides on the product roadmap and ranks features—what to do when, for the program. The project portfolio team decides when to commit to a project or a program.

These teams work from their perspective—feature team, product, or organization—when they make decisions.

The product owners across the program work as a product value team, or a product owner team. When they work across the organization, they can limit the number of interdependencies and continue to update the roadmap based on what the teams complete.

Anyone with product owner in his/her title must understand the value of the feature under discussion, and the customer base for this product. If a product owner doesn't understand the customer base for this product, the PO will not make good decisions based on value. The PO will not be able to answer any of the questions about risk, such as, "What do our customers need or want?" for this product.

The product owner must also understand the product technology. If the PO understands the technology, the team can explain, "We can do things this way or that way." Or, "If we implement this feature first, we can save time on that feature second." Or, "We can implement the flow this way and save time for the user." See the discussion at Product Manager vs. Product Owner.[1]

When the PO understands the customers and the technology, you have a great PO. Without both, you miss the boat.

The product owners on the teams know where the product is. They can see the product evolve every day. They have the responsibility to make small decisions *every day* that help the product grow.

Use the intelligence of the product owners as a team to create and update the agile roadmap. The smaller the features are, the easier this is.

If you have the PPO attempt to dictate the product direction without feedback, this becomes quite difficult. Your program will lose momentum. If the all the product owners join in collaboration with the PPO to create the agile roadmap and the release definition, based on what they've decided the teams should deliver, your program will maintain its momentum.

---

[1] http://svpg.com/product-manager-vs-product-owner/

3.4 **Organize the Software Program Team**

Now that you have a core team, let's see what your software program team might look like. You might need to review the image What Your Software Program Might Look Like (page 19).

The software program team has feature teams alone, if they can be alone. Joe, Tim, and Henry all have stand-alone feature teams.

If more than one team works on a feature set, you might need a program for that feature set. Collect those teams into a program. Sally has a small program of collected feature teams.

For a software program, scale *out*, not up. There is no hierarchy of project managers, unless the teams desire it. There is no hierarchy of Scrum Masters. The teams are equal and work together.

The software program team has these responsibilities during the program:

- Solve cross-functional technical problems.
- Review, monitor, and manage risks in the feature teams.
- Solve problems that escalate from the feature teams.
- Monitor product status.
- Clear program obstacles for the teams.
- Provide consulting to the core team about risks, product decisions, and more.

The software program team does not have to get large. When I run programs, I email the program team meeting agenda (a problem solving meeting) to everyone on the program, and say, "Here are the people I need to attend. Everyone else: let me know if you are attending."

Avoid Coordination Chaos

If everyone has to participate in every meeting, your program will never deliver a product.

If you have 20, 30, or 40 teams, ask the feature teams to organize as "feature set" teams. That will help several teams to become small programs inside the larger program.

Request that one person—the program manager for that feature set—participate in the software program team meetings. That feature set team can then decide how they want to make the information transparent to and from all the feature teams.

You may discover your organization has a natural limit to how big a program can get for the software program or the hardware program. Some managers would like to throw people at the program, in the hopes that they can work faster because there are more people. You may discover that it's so hard to coordinate the communications and interdependencies, it's not worth the bigness. It's worth having the program take longer while using agile roadmaps, so the program teams and the program manager can manage the coordination.

 Every organization has a sweet spot for program size. If you are starting with program management, try to keep your program to nine teams or fewer. Learn how to program-manage at that size before you start with a larger program. You might not need more teams than that.

> ## Do You Need a Hardware Program Team?
>
> You'll notice I mentioned a hardware program team. If you have a product that requires a hardware program team, or a mechanical program team, organize those program teams. Remember, once you have more than a couple of project teams, *consider* organizing a small program for them. My rule of thumb is that once I have four project teams, I have a small program. That's my rule of thumb. Yours might be different.
>
> I consider firmware a special case of software. I also ask that the firmware be updatable just as if it were software. That way, we have the maximum flexibility for release decisions.

3.5 Don't Manage More than One Program Team Yourself

Some program managers whose organizations are transitioning to agile are not always clear about which program team they are managing. Sometimes, that's because the organization doesn't always realize they need more than one program team.

You might think you can manage the core team and the software program team, especially if you only have three to five project teams for the software part of the program. It's tempting.

Don't do it.

You can manage one program team and have one kanban board. Make sure everyone sees all the status, risks, obstacles, everything. Or, you can have two program teams, and you will need to choose which program team you manage.

Once you have three or more teams, they tend to need a program manager of their own. That's a guideline, not a rule. In your program, the software teams might need a program manager for two teams, especially if they are geographically distributed. They have more obstacles and interdependencies.

If you try to manage more than one program team, you will not succeed at facilitating the necessary collaboration across the organization. You will not be a useful servant leader and you will let people down. Don't do it.

3.6 Principles of Organizing Your Program Teams

1. Know which program teams you need. The principles are: "See the whole" and "Simplicity."
2. Your core team, if you need one, is as large as you need it to be, and as small as you can make it. The principle is: "Amplify learning."
3. Make sure the core team consists of everyone you need to release the product. The principle is: "Business people and developers must work together."

CHAPTER 4

Start Your Program Right

If you want your program to succeed, start in a way that promotes success. Use a program charter to define the vision and what done means for the entire program. In addition, create the first agile roadmap to show everyone the big picture, the product direction.

4.1 A Program Charter Sets the Strategy

Starting a program is a lot like starting a project. You need to know where you're going. You need to know what done means. That means you need a program charter. Chartering a program creates a shared vision for the program team and by extension, the entire program.

A program charter's scope is the entire product. Imagine your product is a web site that allows people to buy antiques. There is a search project that allows people to search and place items on wishlists; email to notify the potential buyer of new or existing products; and a transaction processing project that helps people pay for what they want.

The program charter might be something like this: "Provide antique lovers a way to buy unusual items, personalized for their tastes." That vision infers the search, communication, and payment projects, but doesn't say anything about the specific projects in the program. The program vision helps people see entire-product possibilities.

When the program team creates a charter, they have a chance to coalesce, to work as a program team. That's because they learn to define and agree on the project's purpose, vision, and release criteria. By the time the program team finishes the charter, they understand where the program is headed and what done means for the program.

For projects, chartering has the same effect. A project charter limits its scope to a feature set, even if the feature set is large. If you have email as part of your product, the project team that implements email will limit its vision to email. And, a project team (or several small teams) can work together to write a project charter.

Once your program has more than about three teams, you may not want everyone on the program (core team, software program team, and feature teams) participating in the program chartering effort—that's too many people.

No matter how you decide to involve people, charter the program. The program charter sets the stage for the entire program. If necessary, each project can write its own charter based on the program.

The charter helps everyone understand what the program needs from them and how they can contribute. They can make the little decisions and tradeoffs every day that add up.

Ordinarily, you bring your program team together in one room to create the charter. But, what happens when your program is big? Or, it's geographically distributed? Or, you don't even know who is supposed to be on which program team? This is when program management demonstrates its value—when circumstances are not easy.

4.2 Develop the Program Charter with the Core Team

The core team is responsible for the business value of the program. The charter defines why the organization is working on the program, and explains the reasons for the subordinate plans: marketing plan, the sales plan, the training plan, the deployment plan, and on and on.

The core team is responsible for the program charter. If your program is limited to say, 25 people or fewer, you might want to bring all of the people together to charter the program—as long as an experienced facilitator runs that meeting.

If your organization has told 150 people to start this program on Monday, do not try to create a program charter with *everyone*. It's quite difficult—if not impossible—to facilitate 150 people to embrace one vision and release criteria.

You need enough people to collaborate on the program charter so you get feedback from the people working on the program. You need to keep that number small enough so that you can facilitate the people in the room.

For a program, especially if you have distributed teams, I recommend you get everyone on the core team in one physical location to create the charter. If someone says, "We don't have the budget," see the ideas in We Can't Afford the Travel.

4.3 We Can't Afford the Travel

It's time to charter the program, and you're all separated by time zone. Your manager says no, the organization can't afford the travel.

Because the program is a large effort, everyone needs to be hyper-aware of expenses and, as a result, budget wisely. That's why getting everyone together in one physical location to charter the program, develop the initial product roadmap, and determine what you need in a first release is so cost-effective.

Initiating planning with the entire program team can help.

Here's how you sell the idea to your management. How much would it cost for each person to come to one location for a week? Average out the costs for every person on your program team. Let's assume you have ten people on your program team and the average cost is $3000 for a week of travel. That's $30,000.

Now, what are the costs for every week of program delay? If you assume people cost $75/loaded labor hour, then a one-week delay on your project would be $75 multiplied by the number of people multiplied by 40 (hours in a week). You could easily have a one-week delay if people on the feature teams don't know what they are supposed to do when.

How many people do you have on your program now? If it's 25 people, the cost of a one-week delay is $75,000. If it's 80 people, that number is $240,000. If it's 150 people, that number is $450,000, for just one week of delay.

Compare that cost to starting the program right, doing some initial backlog preparation, bringing the program team together to prepare for influencing each other, all that relationship-building? Priceless. Certainly cheap compared to travel costs.

Remember, you can pay for inexpensive travel now or defects and confusion that causes a large Cost of Delay later. Your choice.

4.4 Lead the Program Chartering Effort

The core team is responsible for the charter. As the program manager, you can lead the program chartering effort. You cannot and do not want to write the program charter alone. If you write the charter alone, you lose the opportunity to help the core team coalesce as a team.

"Working Agreements Helped Us Charter"

We were all accustomed to working on smaller agile projects—one, maybe two teams. Then we had to start this large program. We tried to write a charter, and got stuck.

We all knew how to work in agile teams, different agile teams. We did not know how to work together. We decided to develop our working agreements as a core team.

Once we had working agreements, we were able to charter. Our working agreements helped us see how to work together across the organization.

—Experienced agile project manager,
transitioning to a core team program manager

Start the program with the core team a few days before you invite the rest of the feature teams. If you already have the feature teams on board, I ask the feature teams to learn how to work together for one iteration, as in How to Start a Program With More People Than You Need (page 161). That gives the core team a chance to learn how to work together and create the program charter.

For a program, make sure the charter is visible. I like to write the charter, post it, and make it available so everyone on the program can see it whenever they need to. In a sense, the charter is one of your Big Visible Charts, even though it is not something you measure. After all, the reason to charter the program is to make sure everyone understands why they are spending their time working on this endeavor.

4.5 Create Your Own Program Charter Template

At a minimum, the program charter contains the product vision and release criteria, so people know why they are working on the program, and how they will know when they can release the final version of the product.

You may want to add major milestones such as trade shows or target dates; what is driving this program, ROT07, and pointers to other plans or the risk list.

Agile Program Charter Template: Start here and make it yours

1. Product vision: Why does the organization want the product?

2. Release criteria or acceptance criteria: How you know the product is done.

3. Major dates with program implications, such as demos or target release date.

4. Product Roadmap or pointer to it

5. Pointer to other plans: Deployment plan, Sales plan, Training plan, etc.

6. You may need a pointer to the program risk list.

Remember: You can always add more. But, people do not read long documents.

Figure 4.1: Agile Program Charter Template

This charter is both a charter document and a program plan. If you need to break the document into two, consider having just the vision and release criteria as the program charter document. You can then have the rest of the document as the program plan.

If you have one document as your program charter, you can workshop the program charter with the entire core team in one day or less at the beginning of the program. I recommend this because it's easy and helps the core team coalesce as a team.

4.5.1 *Develop the Program Vision*

The product vision helps the core team create the program roadmap and the program backlog. It also helps the feature teams make decisions daily. The program vision may even help the projects create their visions, if necessary.

Here are three steps to creating a program vision:

1. Define the primary customers for this product. They could be the mass market, existing customers, new customers, or a specific market segment.
2. Define the benefit of the program. Why are you doing this program? Answer the "why" question.
3. Define the problems this product solves.

Write as much as you need to, and then edit until you're down to two to four sentences. If your vision is longer than four sentences, you haven't described the program focus yet.

As the core team works through these issues, they will become more of a team. You will uncover risks at the beginning of the program. See Identify program risks (page 43) for more information about risks.

If you have a small program, and everyone is in the room, you might ask people to split into small groups of threes or fours, and work on this in parallel.

Timebox this to 30 minutes. You might not create the perfect vision. You can iterate on this after you do the next piece, the release criteria.

4.5.2 *Develop Release Criteria*

Release criteria tell you what "done" means for the program. You cannot list all the features—that would be impossible. You might have a few scenarios of what the product should be able to do. Maybe you have a target date in mind. Maybe you have some performance criteria in mind.

Release criteria are the vital few criteria that tell you when the product is done, ROT07. They are not everything you could do in the product. As long as you remember that, you'll be fine.

Do You Need Landing Zones?

Sometimes, you have to make technical tradeoffs when you start a program. You *almost* know what done means, but not quite. Those tradeoffs provide you a landing zone.

Imagine a smartphone. You know the product developers will need to trade off battery size with performance consumption, heat dissipation, where the antenna is, and probably other things I don't know about. That's what I mean by landing zone.

Note your landing zones in your charter. Note how you will resolve the zones during the program. Make sure the resolution is on the roadmap somewhere.

If you add landing zones, describe them in a way that makes sense to the feature teams. You may say, "We need landing zones that trade off power consumption and battery life" for a hardware product. For a software-only product, you might say, "We need landing zones that trade off database performance and footprint."

4.5.3 *Major dates*

If you have major milestones, this is the place to put them. Maybe you have a trade show. Maybe you have monthly drops from a vendor or to a vendor/customer. Maybe you have to meet a regulation. Whatever it is, make sure you have transparent dates.

Specify Neutral Dates

A US-based core team program manager wrote down the major dates for his program as 6/1/2014, 8/2/2014, and 10/15/2014. Those dates meant June 1, 2014; August 2, 2014, and October 15, 2014.

When the UK-based software program team manager saw the dates, she was concerned. "Why do we have dates that are so close together? You have 6th Jan, 8th Feb, and what is the 15th month anyway? I have no idea what you mean."

The UK-based program manager suspected the dates were in month/day/year order. She needed to check. Sure enough, they were. Based on her surprise, the core team program manager decided to spell out all dates. He didn't put the day first, but because he specified the month in spelling, not numbers, everyone else understood what he meant.

Consider neutral dates the larger and more geographically distributed your program is.

4.5.4 *Point to the product roadmap*

Your product owners or the program product owner will create and deliver a product roadmap to the program. However, you and the core team and/or the program team might have to collaborate to create the first roadmap to show everyone the product direction. (See Create the Agile Roadmap (page 44) for details about how to create a roadmap.)

4.5.5 *Develop the other plans*

After you create the program vision and release criteria, the other program team members can produce their plans for their areas. Those plans are deliverables to the core team.

Your first job might be to create a kanban where the deliverables are the project plans for the core team. Everyone who is a delegate to the core team owes the core team a plan for their work. Otherwise, why do they need to be on the core team? I find this is a great way to get people off the program team who "just" want to visit. It's okay if they want to visit. They can watch, and not talk. They don't get to problem-solve or participate. The entry into any program team is a plan.

Ask the program team members to keep their project plans short. The plans are action-item based: what this function needs to deliver for the program so that the product can release. That's it.

4.5.6 Identify program risks

You might know of significant risks to your program at the start. If you do, develop your risk list and mitigation plans now—as much as you can.

Numbered Risk	Risk Description	Probability	Severity	Exposure	Trigger Date	Mitigation Plan
Number each risk	Name the risk with a phrase or sentence	Probability the risk will occur	The severity if the risk occurs	Multiply the probability times severity	Date by which you need to act	Plan to deal with the risk
1	The potential problem	High, medium or low	High, medium or low	(M, H)	Make sure this date is not too late to solve the potential problem.	Say as much as you need to so your readers understand your plan.

Figure 4.2: Program Risk Template

I recommend you use high, medium, and low to describe your risks. Many programs start with significant pieces of undefined risks. If you try to describe them with percentages, you might encounter these problems:

- Other people, such as senior managers, want to reduce the significance of the risks by reducing the number percentage.

That provides people with emotional relief but not risk management.

- Using numbers at the start of the program leads people to believe you have more data than you do. One senior developer once said to me, "I thought that was only a 60% problem." It wasn't.

Consider brainstorming the list of risks you want to manage and mitigate with your program team. That way, you can see risks at the business level with the core team, and the risks at the technical level with the software program team.

4.6 Iterate on the Program Charter and Plans

It's better for your program to have a partial charter of the product vision and the release criteria than to wait and have a "complete" charter. When you iterate, you show the people on your program how to build incrementally and iterate. The program team provides the example of working in an agile and lean way.

Don't be afraid to iterate on the charter because nobody knows everything at the beginning of the program. Your program team needs time to learn, as much as the feature teams do.

Do not use an Iteration Zero to build the necessary documentation. If you allow two weeks, it will take two weeks. However, if you organize the program team and create a workshop to build the vision and release criteria, the program team members will know enough to generate the first draft of their plans. You can help the program be more agile by asking people to iterate on their plans.

4.7 Create the Agile Roadmap

The product vision is necessary but not sufficient to start your program right. In addition to the charter, use this time to create the first agile roadmap.

The agile roadmap provides product direction to everyone: the product development teams, the program teams, and the sponsors. The agile roadmap explains the product direction. The product direction provides context to everyone.

A roadmap is a wish-list, what you want to occur. Backlogs are what the teams do. As the teams finish their backlogs, the product owners update the roadmap.

The roadmap has the internal and external releases, the feature sets (also called themes), and when the product owners hope to see features in the product. It's a roadmap; it's what you *hope* the teams can implement.

 The roadmap is a wish-list. It is not a promise to fulfill. The roadmap is a product direction.

Just like a regular map, the teams may encounter detours along the way. That's why the product owners create ranked backlogs for the teams that are much smaller in scope. The product owners update the roadmap based on reality, just as you would if you were driving somewhere and encountered a detour.

Make sure your roadmap is enough for your program to look ahead. If you don't need a six-quarter perspective, consider a six-month perspective. One organization I know has three-month programs. They use a 12-week perspective. They have multiple teams, so they need to show everyone approximately when the teams need to deliver what. But their perspective is the entire program. See Figure 4.3 on page 46.

As the teams complete features, the product owners update the roadmap for this quarter. If the teams deliver at least monthly, the product owners can update the quarter-by-quarter roadmap each month. The product owners update both roadmaps when they need to make decisions or change the product decisions.

The backlogs will change even if the roadmap doesn't. Develop the detailed backlogs for at least one and no more than three iterations. If your teams use kanban, develop several more features than a team would see on its kanban board.

The more prep work you do for the backlogs, the more you will discover you will waste time. The teams need to know which features

Agile Roadmap for a Product: Several Quarters Out

Q1	Q2	Q3	Q4	Q5	Q6

| External Release Tulip | External Release Daisy | External Release Rose | External Release Carnation | | |

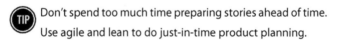

Int. Release 1	Int. Release 2	Int. Release 3							
Feature Sets/ Themes	Feature Sets/ Themes	Feature Sets/ Themes	Feature Sets/ Themes	Feature Sets/ Themes	Feature Sets/ Themes	Feature Sets/ Themes	Feature Sets/ Themes	Feature Sets/ Themes	Feature Sets/ Themes
Feature Sets/ Themes	Feature Sets/ Themes	Feature Sets/ Themes	Feature Sets/ Themes	Feature Sets/ Themes	Feature Sets/ Themes	Feature Sets/ Themes	Feature Sets/ Themes	Feature Sets/ Themes	Feature Sets/ Themes
Feature Sets/ Themes	Feature Sets/ Themes	Feature Sets/ Themes	Feature Sets/ Themes	Feature Sets/ Themes	Feature Sets/ Themes	Feature Sets/ Themes	Feature Sets/ Themes	Feature Sets/ Themes	Feature Sets/ Themes

Figure 4.3: A Potential Agile Roadmap

they will work on next. The roadmap helps the teams see the overall product direction.

> **TIP** Don't spend too much time preparing stories ahead of time.
> Use agile and lean to do just-in-time product planning.

Defining and updating the roadmap takes time. Defining small features, ranking them, and re-ranking them also takes time. Your product owners will discover it's a fine line between providing the teams a long-term perspective (the roadmap) and creating waste because what the teams implement from the backlogs will change the long-term perspective and the next backlog.

This fine line is why each team's product owner role is a full-time job. It's not possible for a product owner to weave in and out on an agile program and expect to satisfy the role. They can't. The teams need their product owners full time to prepare stories for the next ranked backlog. The product owner will need to answer questions and provide feedback about the stories they are working on now.

Product ownership on a program is full-time job. See The Product Owner Role Is Key to the Program's Success (page 27).

4.8 Create the Big Picture Roadmap

You can put features, feature sets, themes, or epics into your roadmap. You might also like to add external milestones into the big picture roadmap, so people understand what you need and when. It will depend on how much you already understand about the problem you need to solve and the duration of your program.

A *feature set* is a collection of related features in one area of the product. A feature set might be:

- Several stories about login and security, all specified as stories so that you can see their value.
- They would include what can go wrong with login, such as malicious users.
- They would include how to create a new user, how to send a password to someone who has forgotten a password, and so on.
- They would be ranked, so the PO can decide which of those features to do now and which ones to do later.

A *theme* or an *epic* is a high-level statement of what you want for a feature. It is a promise to create stories. A theme might be:

- Do electronic signature.
- Do security for login.
- Password reset.

Stories have a value as part of their definition. A theme talks only about the features and not much about the benefits. Do you see the difference in specificity?

The product owner might start with themes, and evolve them to feature sets. Take the time for a requirements workshop or user story mapping to fully specify the feature sets. Then the PO can rank the feature sets to decide which stories in the feature set the team will implement now and which stories the team will implement later.

This is an example of what your one-quarter roadmap might look like.

Product Example: One Quarter Agile Roadmap

Internal Release 1		Internal Release 2		Internal Release 3	
Secure Login, Part 1	Secure Login, Part 1	Secure Login, New ID	Text Transfer, Part 1	Text Transfer, Part 1	Secure Login, Part 3
Admin, Part 1	Diagnostics, Part 1	Admin, Part 2	Admin, Part 2	Admin, Part 2	Admin, Part 2
File Transfer, Part 1	File Transfer, Part 1	Engine, Part 1	Engine, Part 1	Engine, Part 2	Engine, Part 2

Figure 4.4: Example of an Agile Roadmap for One Quarter

For the first internal release, the login team would do secure login, part 1. The admin team would do Admin, Part 1 and Diagnostics, Part 1. The platform team would do File Transfer, Part 1.

Because the teams complete their stories, the product owner can decide which feature set, or part of a feature set you want when. The product owners can guide the teams to creating a walking skeleton in order of value.

4.9 Principles of Start Your Program Right

1. Spend enough time chartering, so you know where the program has to go. Don't spend so much time that you don't start

delivering. The principle is: "Deliver early and often to satisfy the customer."

2. Ask the technical teams for feedback on the vision and release criteria. Do they understand those pieces of the charter? Are those pieces clear enough for the technical teams to make tradeoffs? The principles are: "Empower the team" and "See the whole."

3. Start with a high-level, big picture of your roadmap. Keep evolving that picture, so people can see where you want the product to go. The principle is: "Business people and developers must work together."

CHAPTER 5

Use Continuous Planning

You've seen how to create your first roadmap and maybe even the first couple of product backlogs for any given team. Now, consider how you will update the roadmap and backlogs.

As you replan, consider how small you can make the features and minimum viable products. Your program will increase its throughput as the batch size remains small.

5.1 Differentiate Between Internal and External Releases

If you have continuous delivery, you can deliver something internally, to your organization, every day or multiple times a day. If you don't have continuous delivery, you might not be able to release every day.

Release something internally to your organization at least once a month. Releasing that often provides the entire program with feedback. It also provides a cadence that others will find dependable. When you release internally, you build trust across the organization. It makes sense to release as often as possible.

Internal releases help the feature teams to obtain feedback about the product. The internal releases will also show your management and sponsors the value of your work. Internal releases show people inside the organization what you have completed.

External releases show your customers what you have done. External releases are a business decision. Maybe your customer can take the updated product now, maybe not. However, the teams still need feedback on their work more often than once a quarter or whenever your customer can take a release. This is why you need internal releases at least as often as once a month.

You can release internally more often than once a month. Make the once-a-month the *minimum* time between internal releases.

5.2 What Do You Want to Release This Month?

Teams need small features so they can integrate and release often. Even though you want to release something every month, it will be small. What do you want to release this month?

Let's assume you have two-week iterations. Two two-week iterations fit into one month. If you work in three-week iterations, you could release at the end of each iteration. If you work in flow, maybe you want to release every time you complete a feature, instead of two weeks. Maybe you want to release when you have a minimum viable product (MVP).

I assume you release internally *at least* as often as once a month. More often is great. The more often you release internally, the more everyone—the program participants, your sponsors, anyone interested in your program—can see your progress. Everyone sees feedback.

The less often you release, the more the feature teams have to estimate. With more internal releases, the product owners can change the backlogs. It's a win-win.

 Create internal releases so everyone can see program progress. The larger the program, the more you need frequent internal releases.

If you use continuous delivery, you might not need the one-quarter agile roadmap as in Example of an Agile Roadmap for One Quarter on page 48. Your program would release features faster than a product owner could maintain the roadmap.

Consider the lack of frequent-enough delivery an impediment. See if the feature teams can solve this problem, or if it is a program issue.

5.3 Create Minimum Releasables

From the big roadmap, you can generate something that allows you to see what your minimum viable products, your MVPs, are for each internal release.

Maybe the product owners for a given feature set say something like this, "We don't have something minimum unless at least 80% of the features exist." They are correct when they consider an *external* release. However, your program needs minimum *internal* releases.

Maybe instead of a minimum viable product, the product owners can consider a *Minimal Indispensable Feature Set*, MIFS (BRO14).

MVPs or MIFS will vary in size. Each feature set might need something different for an MVP.

"Our Product Grew Differently Over Time"

We had an email system as part of our product. We had an MVP of basic get-and-send emails in our first MVP. But, we didn't do forwarding or attachments until our second internal release. We didn't do group emails until our third internal release. We took other features from other feature sets, even though we were the "email" team.

I was surprised that the team didn't have such a difficult time with that. I had a harder time because I was the product owner. I wanted to finish the email system, already! But, the team saw where the product roadmap was going, and it made sense to them. They were okay with doing different features, and they had fun with it.

They called themselves the "Email and... Team," because they did email and lots of other features. They said that knowing their MVPs made a difference for them.

—A feature team product owner

Do not try to plan specifics of the feature sets/themes for more than one quarter at a time. Even one-quarter is a ton of planning. Note that you need to consider your MVPs for release.

If you restrict your planning to the MVPs for the internal releases for a quarter: what has to be in your MVPs for each internal release each quarter and then work towards that, you will do enough planning for most projects.

If you release something every month, you never have to do big release planning. If you update the agile roadmap every iteration, or after every few features when teams work in flow, you can direct the product development without big release planning. It's all about MVPs, minimum viable product. As long as you select your MVP for the feature set, or for the entire product, and create small stories, the teams will work towards that.

Continuous Delivery and Quarterly Planning

If you use continuous delivery, do you still need quarterly planning? You might.

If you need to commit across the organization or to customers, use a roadmap. The roadmap will show people the small items for product direction now, and the larger items later. Everyone can see the product direction.

The fact that you do continuous delivery makes it much easier to deliver as needed and to commit to those predicted deliverables.

The roadmap is a wish-list. The deliverables are the reality.

5.4 Plan for External Releases

If the product owners always define MVPs, and the teams always deliver MVPs, and the MVPs move the product towards the release criteria, no one has to worry about what goes into external releases.

If you have continuous delivery, you don't have to worry about external releases. You release all the time.

You have to worry about external releases when:

- The program doesn't release all the time.
- The feature teams don't do continuous integration and release what they have into the mainline.
- Teams work on architecture as opposed to features (when the feature teams don't create features).

If you get caught in these traps, the program has problems. Either the teams have problems at the team level, or the entire program has problems. The product owners can start addressing these problems by creating MVPs and making sure the teams deliver value, not architectural stories.

5.5 Deliverable and Rolling Wave Planning Helps

Internal releases are deliverable-based planning. The product owners specify the deliverable chunks they want to see. As the teams finish the chunks, they can take more.

Rolling wave scheduling is this:

- Schedule your next deliverable. Make sure that deliverable is no longer than two to four weeks away.
- At the end of your first week, schedule the next deliverable.
- Repeat, after each week.

Now you always have a two-to-four week schedule with deliverables.

The teams can use iterations or flow. It doesn't matter. Each team has this responsibility: provide a constant flow of value without incurring technical debt. See Continuous Integration and Testing Supports Collaboration (page 85) for more information about ways to remove technical debt.

You or the program product owner might decide that the program can take some technical debt to meet a specific deliverable. (I don't recommend this.) As part of your deliverable-based planning, add the resolution of that debt to the product roadmap or a future backlog.

Using rolling wave budgeting and incremental budgeting is especially helpful if you have people who want to know how much the project will cost. You can update the spend and plan numbers with every release.

5.6 Small is Beautiful for Programs

Some people think as you create an agile and lean program, it's difficult to have short iterations. They tell me that because more people and teams are on the program, you need to make the iterations longer.

The problem is this: the more you want the benefits of agile or lean, the more you need feedback. The larger the program, the more frequently you need feedback. Why? You do not want to drive the company under while it is waiting for you to complete the program. The longer it takes to get feedback on any feature or set of features, the more difficult it is for the company to know whether the program is succeeding.

The larger the program, the more the organization spends on your work. You need to deliver—at every level—often. The value of making progress every day is that everyone gets feedback. People learn early if anyone is going down the wrong path. You don't have the opportunity to bankrupt your organization because you are not delivering.

If you Review the Twelve Principles of Agile Software Development (page 2), and Review the Seven Lean Principles (page 3), you can see that the principles are about delivering working software, as fast as possible. Shorter iterations allow you to do that.

What if the people on your teams think that short iterations encompass overhead for planning and estimation and, even retrospectives? There are several reasons for that.

- When you hear the word "overhead," you are hearing someone who has not yet fully transitioned to agile. Overhead is code for "we have impediments, and we don't yet realize what they are, so we call them overhead." These impediments might be large stories, and the lack of understanding that they can spike a large story to break it into smaller chunks; or it could be a misunderstanding of what a minimum viable product could be.
- Those folks might not realize how little planning they need to do, to complete small deliverables and achieve an internal release each month.
- If your organization has not yet started to manage the project portfolio, people are multitasking among several projects or features. Under those conditions, you will have trouble building and maintaining a program of small features.
- You have a complex product, so the teams extend their iterations to more than two weeks to achieve some form of an MVP. I'll talk more about this in Shepherd the Architecture (page 143).

What if *you* think the iterations need to be longer? If you think planning is overhead, I bet you don't have small stories, or that you are trying to use estimation to manage the product roadmap or the project portfolio.

Start thinking about value. Start thinking about the smallest feature that will show everyone the progress of a feature or feature set.

5.7 How Often Can You Replan?

Continuous planning works in much the same way as continuous integration. When the feature teams integrate all the time, code integration is easier. When you replan all the time, the planning takes less time and is easier.

When you use continuous planning, you don't have to have big plans. You can plan for the next iteration (or two). You can plan for the next deliverable (or two). You never have to have everyone in the same room for release planning.

As the product owners see and accept the features that the teams complete in their backlogs, they can update the roadmap as a product value team. Continuous planning avoids the need for a large "let's get everyone in the same room" to plan a quarter's worth of work.

Very few teams can plan for a quarter at a time and meet that plan. Your program might have interruptions from operations/support, the rank of some features might change, and teams encounter problems every day. If you plan for a quarter, you are not likely to accomplish everything you plan.

With continuous planning, you update the backlogs just in time and keep your program open to change. The smaller your planning, the more likely the teams are to be able to achieve the vision and release criteria.

 Keep planning small. With small stories, small planning, and small teams, your program is more likely to have faster throughput and faster feedback. Small and frequent planning helps your program be more resilient.

The more you can move to continuous planning, the more agile and lean your program will be. The point of the roadmaps is to show the team the big picture of the product, and how that vision changes over time. The backlogs are the specifics for each team.

The more risk you have in your program, the more feedback you need. The more you want to keep the sponsors engaged, the more often you might have to change the roadmap—and by extension—the backlogs.

If you want more feedback, release more often. Can you release every day? If not every day, what impediments do you have for creating an internal release at least once a month? As a program manager, remove those impediments. Then you can ask the program product owner to update the roadmap at least as often as once a month.

"It's not the Plan; It's About Planning"

I used to use a more waterfall approach to my programs. I tried to plan once and have it be "the plan of record" for the entire program.

It didn't work so well. I was always replanning. Then I discovered rolling wave planning, and I learned about the value of *planning*, where we discussed what we could do when, and where the risks were, versus the actual plan, which was always out of date the next day.

Now, I use our planning as a way to understand problems and risks. I use the planning to help make decisions over the next few weeks. I never expect the plan to last past a couple of weeks. But I'm in better shape because of the risk discussions we had.

—A senior program manager

Good planning, in the sense of providing a roadmap for the teams and reflecting the current reality depends on more feedback, not less. When you plan less often, you don't see your current reality. The plans become targets, instead of plans the teams can use to guide their work.

5.8 Separate the Product Roadmap from the Project Portfolio

The larger your program, the more you might have projects in the form of feature sets to sequence. I like to think of this ranking as a form of feature portfolio management. The sequencing occurs when you say something like this, "We need to work on enough features for the Engine before we get to the Diagnostics module or the Finance module."

That might be exactly the right way to approach what is most valuable for the program and your sponsors. That is a form of project portfolio management. However, it is deciding what is right for *this* product, not for the organization overall. Because it is for this product, it's not project portfolio management. (See *Manage Your Project Portfolio: Increase Your Capacity and Finish More Projects*, ROT09 for more information about an organization-wide approach to sequencing projects and programs.)

The product owner value team ranks features and possibly projects (as collections of feature sets) for your program. Do that, and leave the overall project portfolio management to the people who decide on the strategy for your organization.

5.9 Ways to Rank Items in the Roadmap or Backlogs

Do you ever wonder how the product owner or the program product owner decides what to do first, second, or third? As a program manager, you might be able to help the product owner team decide what to do when.

5.9.1 Do the shortest work first

Many product owners like to use schedule estimation as a way to define a value for the features or feature sets. If you decide to do the shortest features first (which might be a great way to be able to show progress), that's called the "weighted shortest job first." See *The Principles of Product Development Flow: Second Generation Lean Product Development*, REI09.

The shortest job first works well when you have dependable estimates and no Cost of Delay. Here are three challenges I have seen to using weighted shortest job first: teams provide inaccurate or long estimates; the teams have interdependencies; or the teams are missing necessary people for them to finish features. In each of these cases, your program will incur a Cost of Delay trying to do the shortest work first. The teams can't tell which work is shortest. Use these other ideas to evaluate items in your roadmap or features in the backlog.

5.9.2 "Is this still valuable?"

What seems like a good idea at the beginning of the program might not be useful at all partway through the program. I recommend that for all features not started—and even the incomplete features—the product owner ask, "Is this still valuable?"

This question is similar to the zeroth question in project portfolio management, "Should we do this project at all?" See *Manage Your Project Portfolio: Increase Your Capacity and Finish More Projects*, ROT09. When you ask this question about the project portfolio, you optimize value for the entire organization. When you ask the value question about the program feature-sets, you optimize the value for this program. You decide which work not to do, which avoids waste.

5.9.3 Use business value points

When I work with clients, I often discover that they know which features are worth more to them and which features are worth less. The problem is they don't know how much more or how much less. Business value points can help.

With these points, you assign a unique number to each feature you consider ranking out of a total number of points. Imagine you have 10,000 points and seven features. Figure 5.2 on page 62 might be your ranking.

The relative value of each feature is what matters. If one team would normally implement all of Features 1, 2, and 3, you can consider asking several teams to work on those features, even if they are not normally the features the teams would implement. That's because those features are so much more important than all the other features *at this time.*

Every time you assess the product backlog, reassign the business value points. One iteration, you might decide you only need 10,000 points. A few iterations later, you might have five more teams and

Feature	Business Value Points
Feature 1	2500
Feature 2	2000
Feature 3	1950
Feature 4	500
Feature 5	250
Feature 6	249
Feature 7	200
Total	7649

Figure 5.2: Ranking with Business Value Points

need to use 50,000 points to decide which parts of which features are most important now. As long as you use a unique number of points, it doesn't matter how many points you use. It matters that each feature has a unique number of points.

5.9.4 Evaluate the Cost of Delay

The Cost of Delay is the cost that the organization incurs when you have delays in the product release. The organization expects to get a benefit from the release. If you delay the product by a month, the cost of that delay is a month of *maximum* lost revenue. The Cost of Delay is real and will slow your program's momentum.

In a program, the teams might encounter many possible causes for a Cost of Delay:

- Waiting for another team to implement a necessary feature.

- Insufficient people on a specific team, e.g., not enough DBAs or testers, or some other scarce person.
- Experts, which lead to queues of work for that person.
- Technical debt.

As part of a program team, you might see delays when people don't finish their actions on time:

- Marketing Communications had a delay with finishing the one-sheets, and there is no point releasing the product without them.
- A vendor doesn't deliver a subsystem on time.
- Hardware is not ready for installation.

There are many possible other causes of Cost of Delay. See *Diving for Hidden Treasures: Finding the Value in Your Project Portfolio* RE14.

Cost of Delay is real. Decide when you need to take the delays into account as you rank features or work for the program.

5.9.5 *Who has waste?*

If you are managing a program that automates some piece of work, the people doing the work have waste until you implement the necessary chunks. I once worked with a program implementing the back office application for a bank. Because the "back end" wasn't done, the back-office people had to manually take the input from the "open a checking account" feature and enter the data into the back-end processing. There was no point in implementing more "front office" features until the back end was complete.

You may have a program in which people have traditionally thought in terms of the "front end" and the "back end." If you do, you may well see waste in all kinds of places in your product. Help people think of features as end-to-end, not front- or back-ends. Thinking this way could be a major change for them. People need time to think in a new way.

Sometimes, waste is part of technical debt. If the teams don't have sufficient automated tests, they "waste" time doing manual testing. I am not saying exploratory testing is a waste. I am saying that tests you run more than once to provide yourself assurance that nothing broke should be automated. That lack of automation is waste.

Teams new to agile may well have test-automation-and-build waste. The earlier you discover this, the better, whether you are a product owner or a program manager. Ranking that work is as important as ranking features.

5.9.6 *What will we learn?*

Sometimes, the program needs to learn about a feature set or several features sets. Sometimes, a team needs to evaluate several options for a user interface. Sometimes, the architects need to experiment with architecture or design to evaluate options. In these cases, you trade early learning against finishing other features.

Do not mistake this learning for "Iteration Zero." Iteration Zero is when you get ready (and get ready and get ready) to start work. Instead, when you schedule learning for a team, timebox the learning and be ready to show the rest of the program the results. The team might not be able to integrate some code. But they should be able to answer questions.

5.9.7 *What risks does this feature manage?*

Your program may have customer-based risks, architectural risks, development risks, and more. If you are sure your customers will be perturbed unless you add this feature and soon, rank that feature higher than others.

I often find that these risks affect each other. The customer wants something right away. Doing that feature puts the rest of the program at risk for delay. There seems to be no right answer. If you see this in your program, try Cost of Delay for your feature ranking. You may have customers who want different features now, or you need to trade off some architectural exploration before you can decide. Cost of Delay may help your decision.

5.10 Decide How You Will Evaluate Value

Use a combination of these evaluation approaches as you work through the program. You might decide to implement some small features first, to see some quick wins (weighted shortest job first). You might decide to learn with spikes or small prototypes to inform the architecture or design of some features (learning). Sometimes, you look at Cost of Delay to see if teams are waiting for this feature or that story. There is no one right answer for evaluating the items in your roadmap or backlogs.

Do not use *just* the estimate of a given feature or feature set. When you do that, the teams feel under tremendous pressure to deliver that feature or feature set inside their estimate. If the item is large, their estimate is likely to be wrong. The program will incur waste, delays, and possibly technical debt.

Instead, consider how you can share the "what value is this to us now" decision with the teams. They will help you.

5.11 Update the Roadmaps Often

The program product owner will need to update the big picture roadmap *at least* once a quarter. If the feature teams release internally at least once a month, the program product owner can update the roadmap and change the backlogs once a month. If your program can use continuous delivery, you can update the roadmaps at least that often.

That means that the team product owners will need to update the MVPs for the feature team backlogs at least once a month.

Use rolling wave planning and interim deliverables, and you never have to do big planning.

Make your stories small—the product owners need to learn how to do this with their feature teams—and no one has to spend a ton of time planning. Instead, everyone spends time discussing what they want for MVPs and what the product looks like now and should look like in the future.

5.12 **Principles of Continuous Planning**

1. Generate the small picture with your MVP, minimum viable products. The principle is: "Business people and developers must work together."
2. Always start from the roadmaps and move to the backlogs. The principle is: "Amplify learning."
3. Plan small so you can evolve the plan as your reality changes. The principle is: "Welcome changing requirements."
4. Update the plan as the teams complete work and reality changes. The principle is: "Deliver working software frequently."
5. Use what the teams complete to inform the next batch of roadmap and backlogs. The principle is: "Decide as late as possible."

CHAPTER 6

Create an Environment of Delivery

Create a program environment where the culture says, "Deliver" every day, a little bit at a time. If the program teams deliver daily, the feature teams are more likely to do so.

Think of this as your own DevOps culture. DevOps is a way to create teams that know how to build and deploy. The idea is that the team can always build. You make deployment automated and tested. You can do one-click deployments.

Remember, you might have a difference in the "deploy so we can see everything inside our building" and "deploy to customers." Every team needs to be able to deploy anything internally at any time. Deployment to customers is a business decision.

The people on your program teams have plenty of work in their "day" jobs. Sometimes they see the program team work as onerous, additional work. It doesn't matter that the product your program is producing might be the product to save the company. That's irrelevant. They have work back in their function that their manager sees as quite important. Often, the program team work will feel like multitasking to them.

How can you help them work on your program team?

6.1 Visualize Program Team Work

You can help them by visualizing the program team work. I like kanban boards for this, because everyone can see the flow of work through the organization.

Ranked Backlog	In Progress		Risk Management or Mitigation	Decision Needed Post-Action	Waiting: Stuck Items	Done
	Action item analysis	Action item resolution				
	Item and date started. Who is working the item.					
MarComm						
Legal						
Sales						
Deployment						
Hardware						

Figure 6.1: Possible Kanban for a Core Team

The figure Possible Kanban for a Core Team shows what you might use for a kanban for a core team. You still have the Ranked Backlog column. Since this is a core team, every program will have their own unique workflow. At minimum, track the work in the "In Progress" and "Waiting" states. When an item is done, the task goes into the Done column.

This is a *possible* kanban board. You may want to change it. If you have research or analysis states, you would add that to your board. If you have "In Purchasing" as a state, you would add that. Your kanban board reflects your flow.

At the bottom are the swim lanes, where everyone can see which items are in progress by the person working the item. If someone needs help, the entire team can see it.

If you see the work in progress, it's easier to help people understand what, when, and why they need to deliver.

Don't bury the work in meaningless milestones, such as "Beta" or some other milestone. Sure, Beta does mean something to everyone on the program. But what are the tasks everyone needs to deliver to get to that milestone? Do deliverable-based planning to achieve that milestone. Keep the tasks small, something people can accomplish inside of a day or two, so they can deliver their work and not feel as if the program has taken over their lives.

I like physical boards wherever possible, rather than electronic boards. Even if your core team and software program teams are experienced at agile and lean, they might be new at being a core team or a software program team for this product. My guideline for new agile and lean teams is to start with a physical board until their work together becomes natural.

For example, they might want to add avatars to the board, as in *Kanban in Action*, (HAM14). That personalizes the board, and helps people know who is working on what.

6.2 Keep the Program Team Work Small

When you keep the work small, people feel as if they are accomplishing something. That makes them feel good about themselves, and sets them up to do more work. It changes their mindset.

On the other hand, if they slog through a large task, and feel as if it's never-ending, they don't feel good. They are in danger of never completing the work, even if they are minutes away from completion (AMA11). The problem with large tasks is that you might not be able to tell you are minutes away from completion.

When people put small tasks on their kanban boards, they are more likely to take them and finish them. If they put large tasks, such as, "Redo Licensing," they are less likely to take them. If your program team members create large tasks, ask them to break those down into the component tasks. Those tasks might be:

- Call the meeting with sales, support, and legal on Friday.
- Prepare the handout for the meeting with the proposed changes highlighted. Do by Thursday to send out in advance.
- Run decision by CFO after we all agree.

Now, everyone can see that "Redo Licensing" is not trivial. They might make other suggestions, such as, "Should we have Finance in the initial meeting?"

If you keep your program team kanban visible, everyone can see what you are doing. Who knows? Other people might have suggestions, too. When the program team members deliver all the time, the feature teams are more likely to do so, also.

6.3 How Features Flow Through Teams

I've talked a lot about the program teams so far. You might be wondering how the features flow through the teams. If each team is agile, and a fully functional feature team, it's easy.

Feature teams have all the roles they require. Each team is able to deliver a story/feature every day or two days, following these principles:

- Visualize the workflow, so the team can see the value stream, bottlenecks, and any work in progress. Teams do this, in case they become interdependent on another team.
- Keep the batch size (story size) small, as in no larger than two days. Why? This allows everyone to integrate everything all the time. It also allows the entire program to do continuous delivery, even if that delivery is just internal. It also allows for fast feedback and change. Small stories make interdependencies more obvious. It allows you to separate the business decision for product release from the actual decision of release.
- Use good engineering practices such as test-driven development, acceptance test-driven development, unit testing, pairing, whatever you need so that you have a safety net for your development. The technical practices we associate with agile provide a safety net for development and allow everyone to proceed at a sustainable pace. If you don't use the engineering practices, you will build technical debt and wonder why you are

breathless, putting in overtime, never able to do what you want to do.

When the feature teams deliver all the time, they build momentum. It's easy for the entire program to see how to proceed.

6.4 How Often Can You Release Your Product?

You can start by assessing how you could release your product. This is not how often you release your product to your customers now. This is your potential for releases. Your customers might not want to take new product as often as you could release. However, if you could release that often, that might change how you think about your program.

Software as a Service	Boxed Software	Product with Firmware	Product with Hardware or Mechanical components
Continuous			Infrequently
Continuous Deployment: As often as several times a day	Often: But the cost of release is high	Less Often: The cost of release is high	Infrequently: Every release might be a major release

Figure 6.2: Potential for Release Frequency

How expensive is it to release your product? The expense of release will change your business decision about when to release your product.

Separate the business decision of releasing your product from making your software releasable.

That is, the more to the left of the continuum you are, the more you can marry your releases to your iterations or your features, if you prefer. Your project portfolio decisions are easier to make, and they can occur as often as you want, as long as you get to done, every feature or iteration.

The more to the right of the continuum you are, the more you need to separate the business decision of releasing from finishing features or iterations. The more to the right of the continuum, the more important it is to be able to get to done on a regular basis, so you can make good project portfolio decisions. Why? Because you often have money tied up in long-lead item expenses. You have to make decisions early for committing to hardware or non-recurring engineering (NRE) expenses.

Why does this matter for your program?

Your program product owner and core team, the people responsible for the business value of the program, will have to make many decisions on a weekly basis about the risks of the program. The more the technical teams can show progress by releasing, the more data the core team has, the better decisions the core team can make. It is that simple.

If you have a Software as a Service (SaaS) product, and you are not able to release as often as once a day, you have impediments. Do you know what those impediments are? Can you remove them?

6.5 Release Internally, Even with Hardware

As an agile program manager, create a culture of delivery even if you have hardware in your program. You might not be able to release new hardware every month because of the expense. You have another alternative.

When hardware developers create their product, they simulate. They can demonstrate from their simulations. It's possible that only the software people understand those demonstrations, but that's fine. Someone has to understand those demonstrations. Have the hardware people demonstrate their working product to the software people.

Then, the software people get to "demonstrable" instead of releasable until the hardware people make prototype hardware available to the program. Once everyone has prototype hardware, everyone can get to releasable.

Ask everyone to be able to release their part of the product at least once each month, or in the case of software, even more often. That's the internal release on the roadmap. When the hardware folks do the final debug on the hardware, they need the most up-to-date software. Having to wait even two weeks is a two-week delay for your program. You have a linear critical path until the software is ready.

If every team, program team or feature team, works on small chunks of work, they can get to done quickly. See if your teams can use continuous integration. If so, as they integrate and build, they can release their work for feedback. The sooner the testers provide feedback to the developers, the fewer defects you will have overall in the program. The sooner everyone integrates their work, the faster the teams can see if they have problems.

The faster the feedback across the program, the less inadvertent technical debt your program will accumulate.

If everyone releases something every day or so, you can create internal releases each month without too much fuss. It takes Autonomy, Collaboration, and Exploration (page 77) on the part of each team.

6.6 Are You Integrating Chunks or Products From Others?

If you are dependent on vendors to supply chunks of your product, create milestones that show the interdependencies. You can share those interdependencies and update the dates for the milestones as the program proceeds.

Consider whether you want a kanban board or a Gantt chart or both to see the interdependencies. A kanban board helps everyone see all deliverables and the state of those deliverables. If you are working with vendors new to agile, you may need a Gantt chart. Your Gantt chart won't be accurate. However, it will help everyone see the interdependencies and allow you to share dates.

If you can help those vendors provide you their working product at least as often as once a month, you have your monthly internal release.

Use rolling wave planning and deliverable-based milestones. (See Deliverable and Rolling Wave Planning Helps, page 56.) Make sure these vendors provide you working product, not specifications. You might also need specs to make sure everyone delivers their part of the product that works. And, because this is an agile program, you can expect some of the details in the specs to change, as your vendors provide you with interim product.

Don't let your vendors run open-loop; they need to provide working product. Share all the dates with all your vendors. They need to see the interdependencies also.

If you use a Gantt chart don't believe the date, not at the beginning. The Gantt chart's end date is the first date you can't prove you can't meet. You might want 3-point estimation (a PERT chart), or a percentage confidence. (See the estimation discussion in Supply a Three-Date Estimate, page 111.) But, the shape of the Gantt will help everyone see what's going on.

"Gantts Helped Everyone See Deliverables"

I used this approach last year to deliver a brand new business far, far sooner than anyone expected. My key driver and my key selling point was this: we haven't had a good track record with this vendor; we expect them to ship us buggy software; I'd rather find the first batch of bugs 6 weeks in, rather than 6 months in; If they don't deliver us buggy software then... brilliant... we can thank them, we can pat them on the back, we have reassurance; if they do ship us buggy software 6 weeks in then we'll need to sit down and have a long, hard conversation, which is even better than brilliant. The vendor didn't like this suggestion but after the project, once they'd finished earlier than they expected and saved themselves a lot of (non-billable) rework, they said they'd love to continue working that way.

The Gantt view was important because so much of that programme's development work needed to revolve around that Vendor's schedule since it was our core platform.

—*Clarke Ching, Programme Manager* (private communication)

6.7 Manage the Risks of Integration from Other Vendors

Your outside vendor (or internal non-agile team) might have terrific plans to deliver your program their monthly deliverables. They might "yes" you and have no plans to deliver. They might be something in-between.

If you integrate systems from other vendors, manage the risks by building integration time into your backlog and schedule. How much integration time? My guideline is that if a vendor is not agile, ask for monthly deliverables and expect to spend a month integrating the first time. That will provide you data.

What do you do in that month? Your feature teams start integrating the vendor's product. On Day One, they find a show-stopper problem. They can't integrate anything until the vendor fixes that problem. Let's assume you have a great vendor and they provide a fix the next day. Your teams continue to integrate and three days later they find another problem. This continues for several weeks.

Here are some ways to manage the integration risks:

- Create an integration team to manage the vendor relationship, find problems, ask for fixes, and nudge the vendor into sending more frequent updates that work.
- Allow as much time for integration as the vendor has between releases to you. If the vendor releases once a month, allow for one month integration. Now, track the elapsed time spent. Use that data to plan for the next integration.
- Ask the vendor to develop and release in an agile way. If your vendor could release every day or several times a day, could you take the product? If not, what would you have to do?

Never assume you will get a defect-free build from a vendor at any time. Never assume your vendor-supplied build will arrive on time. Many vendors who are waterfall have a difficult time with frequent, defect-free releases. Encourage your vendor and, if it fits for you, offer to help them.

6.8 Create a Culture of Delivery Throughout the Program

In programs, the feature teams will have interconnection points with the rest of the feature teams. Ensure nothing prevents the teams from integrating often and demonstrating informally to anyone who will watch. This allows everyone to create a culture of delivery, so you can get feedback and make sure you are on the right track.

6.9 Principles of Create an Environment of Delivery

1. An environment of delivery helps people see the small wins as they work in the program. The principles are: "Deliver early and often to satisfy the customer" and "Deliver working software frequently."

2. Look for places work can hide and expose that work. The principles are: "Eliminate waste" and "Amplify learning."

3. Make iterations and stories short so everyone can deliver daily. Start with a story size that is no larger than a team day or two team days. That allows each team to integrate into the codebase all the time. Everyone can see the product growing all the time. The entire program delivers. Each small win creates more trust across the organization. The principles are: "Deliver early and often to satisfy the customer," "Welcome changing requirements," "Working software is the primary measure of progress," and "Simplicity."

CHAPTER 7

Encourage Autonomy, Collaboration, and Exploration

Back in A Program is a Strategic Collection of Several Projects (page 4), I explained that program management was not scaling agile, that it was scaling collaboration practices across the program.

First, let's talk about what software is, and how that changes how we think about our practices.

7.1 Software is Learning, Not Construction

Product development—especially software development—is about learning. We uncover requirements as we proceed. If you expect to uncover requirements, you will learn as you proceed. Agile and lean allow you to implement and replan as you learn.

We can't build software the same way we construct or manufacture. That's because all new software is innovation.

Software projects help teams learn and innovate as they proceed. We can timebox our learning. We can choose to stop doing something. We can put acceptance or release criteria around it and say, "We have done enough for now."

When I taught a bunch of analog chip designers agile, they said, "This is *exactly* what we do. We iterate until we get the tradeoffs right."

Iterating until you get the tradeoffs right is what you do when you learn.

When you iterate on the design, and build incrementally, you learn throughout the development of your product. You can change as you learn.

Agile and lean approaches assist program management by encouraging change. How? Agile and lean encourage change by helping the teams realize they need to:

- Implement small chunks of work in the form of features.
- Finish that work, so it's done.
- Integrate that work across the program, so everyone sees that work. Retrospect at reasonable intervals.
- Repeat.

It doesn't matter what your product is. It could be an email application, an operating system, an embedded system, or some other product. If you follow the model above, you will learn as you proceed. This learning leads to change. That's where agile approaches are so helpful.

The rate of learning in a program is significant, because there are many more people than there are on a single project. If you try to treat a program as if it is a construction project, you will be disappointed. Do not think you can "roll down" from the program to the projects and be agile. That is hierarchical, waterfall thinking. In agile and lean programs, we scale out from the cross-functional teams.

7.2 Scaling Agile Means Scaling Collaborative Practices

If you want a large program because you want an earlier release date, your teams need to be autonomous, so they can make their own decisions. They need to be collaborative, because they will learn as they proceed. Some of those learnings will create interdependencies. And, the teams need to be able to explore—not open-loop, wander off exploration into nowhere, but exploration with the intent of learning.

The way your program will succeed is if the teams communicate through their tests and continuous integration. It all goes back to the agile and lean principles (See the agile principles, page 2 and the lean principles, page 3) of delivering working software often as a holistic approach.

To encourage speed on your agile program, the program product owner needs to have feature sets on the agile roadmap, not components.

The more specific feature sets you have, the more the teams can create tests and integrate independently. They may still have points of interdependence. However, the more you define specific features inside feature sets, the more the teams can operate as feature teams, or as feature set teams (several teams together working on one feature set).

However, if you want to encourage exploration on your agile program, the program product owner can have themes or epics on the agile roadmap. If your product is brand new, sometimes called "greenfield," you may want to have several feature teams explore together. The feature teams have to work interdependently on each feature.

You may need architects to do some wayfinding, although I prefer that teams do that collaboratively. When teams collaborate on discovering the architecture, they not only produce features now, they also formulate future features for the roadmap.

The larger the feature—the closer it is to a theme or an epic—the slower the feature teams are. They must discuss with each other what the epic means, and what the feature set(s) are for that epic. Teams might have to map their stories together, along with their product owners to understand what the epic is.

If you want speed, the collaborative practices are testing and integration.

If you want exploration, the collaborative practices are story mapping and wayfinding, before you can consider testing and integration.

It depends on how much the product owners and the teams know about the product solution domain.

7.3 Create Autonomous Feature Teams

I assume your program has feature teams, or is working towards composing feature teams. Why? Because your customers buy features.

They don't buy components, unless you sell libraries. They don't buy services. They don't buy architecture or frameworks. They buy features. Consider organizing the teams and what the teams produce by what your customers buy. That way, you can make Conway's Law work for you, not against you. (Conway's Law says the product architecture reflects the communication structures of those organizations. See the Wikipedia entry[1] for more details.)

With a program, if you do not organize by feature teams, each team's Cost of Delay adds up. Single teams think they are done with their work, only to discover later that the components don't create features. See The Teams Have Dependencies on Other Teams (page 189).

If your program is not yet organized into feature teams, take another look at How Features Flow Through Teams (page 70) and the suggestions about moving from other kinds of teams to feature teams. See the ideas in Troubleshooting Agile Team Issues (page 179).

When feature teams are autonomous, they create their own kind of agile approach. It doesn't matter if they use iterations, kanban, both, or neither. It only matters that they have a constant flow of features through their team. If a feature team gets stuck—and this does occur—they can ask for help. But the team needs to be able to create their features by themselves, without relying on experts from another team. Or, without interdependencies with other teams. That's what I mean by autonomous.

Each team can still ask questions of another team or team member. I would expect that. But each team is a fully-functioning agile team, a team which has been practicing, learning, and improving their agile approach.

7.4 Create Small-World Networks to Optimize Learning

What is the "best" way to move information through your organization? The rumor mill.

---

[1] https://en.wikipedia.org/wiki/Conway%27s_law

One person tells someone something. That person tells someone else. It's viral. It's as if the information has a mind of its own. Can you use that network, that viral-ness for the benefit of your program? You can, if you organize the program to do so.

That network has a name. It's called a small-world network. If you have ever used Wikipedia, you used a product created by a small-world network. Anyone can edit Wikipedia. There are some rules, mostly enforced by the community, about how people edit. Wikipedia has the notion of collective "code" ownership. It's natural language, not code, but the ideas are the same.

Most of the users don't change Wikipedia—we see no need to do so. In your program, you would expect the developers to change the code. You would expect the testers to change the tests and the business analysts to change the stories, and so on. You might have some rules about who can change what to make the program environment run smoothly. For example, you might agree on the norm that no one who is not a business analyst or a product owner can change stories less than three weeks out. But, anyone can update for clarity any story at any time.

Small-world networks are flexible and depend on the team members to make them work (*Here Comes Everybody: The Power of Organizing with Organizations*, SHI08). They have almost no limit to their scaling. They don't require hierarchy. They scale out, not up. They have a very low transaction cost. They don't require management. However, they do require that you tell people that you want them to work together.

Figure 7.1 on page 82 is a picture of what one small-world network for nine teams might look like. Your small-world network will be different.

Note that every team is connected to every other team, but not in the same way. Some people are highly connected; some people are much less connected. That doesn't matter. The program can take advantage of how people are connected, even if people are not directly connected to each other.

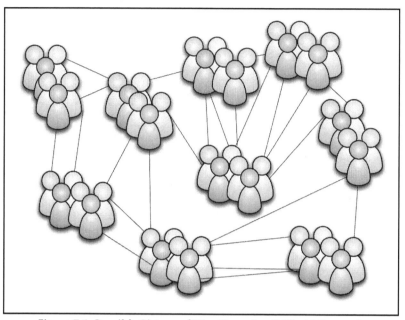

Figure 7.1: Possible Picture of Nine Team Small-World Network

7.5 Communities of Practice Create Connection and Collaboration

When you have feature teams, people want to connect to other people like themselves across the program. They want to connect to other platform, middleware, UI developers. They want to connect to other testers, analysts, writers, DBAs. If you create communities of practice in the program, they will have a way to connect.

The feature teams take responsibility for their features. And, the communities of practice provide people with a way to connect across feature teams and discuss issues that allow them to explore problems and solve them across the program. The communities of practice help people collaborate and learn across the program.

This is an example of what three feature teams might look like if they decided to create communities of practice from their feature teams.

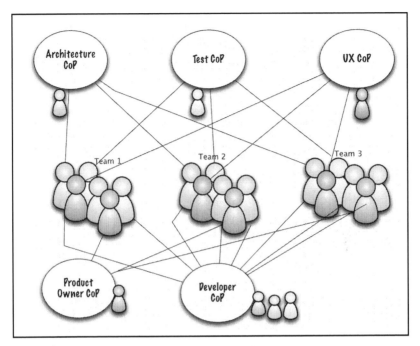

Figure 7.2: Community of Practice

Notice that each community of practice has unique members, except for the Developer community. Because architects are also developers, the architects and developers might overlap. Your program will have to decide what to do: are all developers also architects? Or, are architects, who are embedded on the teams, a subset of the developers? Let the teams decide. Remember, architects guide the business value of the architecture. They are not the only ones allowed to architect. See Shepherd the Agile Architecture (page 143) for more ideas about architects and how they help shepherd the business value of the product.

Communities of practice help the teams connect and decide when and whether to deepen their small-world networks.

This is easier if everyone is collocated. When people are geographically distributed, their opportunities to learn from each other are virtual and not nearly as satisfying. People will still learn from each other when they are distributed. But they may discover it takes longer.

7.6 Avoid Hierarchical Titles

When you start thinking of your agile program as spokes of networks, you realize that the teams move toward not only solving problems themselves but also coordinating among themselves.

 Think of your agile teams as spokes in a wheel. When they all work together, the wheel turns and the program works. When they don't work together, the wheel doesn't turn and gets stuck. No momentum.

I avoid titles such as Chief architect, Chief product owner, Master architect, Über anything, Master anything. The core or the program team members are not part of a hierarchy.

I do use titles such as program manager, program product owner, and when necessary, program architect. The idea behind the program titles is that these people have a responsibility to provide *business value* to the program. They are not hierarchical leaders. They might lead a community of practice as a servant leader, facilitating communication, removing obstacles, connecting people. (See Develop Your Servant Leadership, page 133, for more details.)

However, it is not the program architect's job to do Big Architecture Up Front and design the architecture for the product. On the contrary, it is the program architect's job to nurture the evolution of the architecture and the business value of the architecture as the program proceeds. It is his or her job to worry about the most responsible moment to lead the discussion at the architecture community of practice, "I think we know enough to say this is our architecture for now."

It is the program product owner's job to define the agile roadmap and update it as the program product owner sees the demonstrations and hears from the other product owners in the product owner community of practice.

It is the program manager's job to create the program plan with the core team and update it and the risk list and any other documents if necessary and collaborate across the organization. These program people have extra responsibilities. They are not masters or chiefs or über *anybody*. They have responsibility for business value.

And, if you need a person to be the chief architect, one person to make all the final decisions, say so. That's okay. You might even need one person to be the program product owner (not a chief), to be the person to make the final decision about the roadmap and the backlog. Say so. But make it a transparent decision.

If you're transparent about it, everyone will respect your decision. Your people will appreciate you for your honesty.

7.7 Continuous Integration and Testing Supports Collaboration

I like continuous integration (CI), where each team finishes their small chunks and integrates their work at least once a day. (When I use CI, each team integrates multiple times each day.) It's even better when that small chunk is a story. You don't need hardening sprints. You don't have program-level technical debt. Everyone gets to see the product grow each day.

If you are able to use the product in-house, you can see the product, and get feedback from the in-house users. It's a win for everyone.

Team members can use continuous integration when they automate their unit testing and much of their system testing. Testers will still need to perform the nasty exploratory testing, which will find defects in unexpected places. Testers can automate most of the normal test scenarios that the team needs to run often.

When the teams automate their testing and continuously integrate their code, something magical happens. They can collaborate at the team level because their code works. They can solve problems in their communities of practice and in their small world networks. That has two significant side effects: the program moves faster, maintaining momentum. And, the problems they escalate to the software program team tend to be more difficult to solve.

If the program team solves only the difficult problems, not "how do we transition to agile" problems, the program team can provide optimal value to the program. They solve problems that prevent the entire product from releasing, not the obstacles that prevent your teams from even getting to a product.

If your teams do not have automated tests or are not able to continuously integrate, solve those problems now. Do not wait until you are midway through the program and your product development has stopped because no one can integrate.

In the same way, if the teams do not maintain their automated test development—both unit test and system test development—they will be unable to discover how to fix their code if two features clobber each other. Making features small and using small-world networks helps with collaboration. But maintaining good support for code with test automation and continuous integration helps too.

What can a program manager do?

1. Ask for the result you want. If you want continuous integration, explain that's what you want. I say something like this, "I want the system to be in a releasable state every day. At a minimum, I would like that every week. I know that's not where we are now, and that's the result I would like. What would it take for us to get there?"

2. Assume the technical teams understand the technical problems better than you, the program manager do. If you ask for the problem and impediments, don't poo-poo the problems. Treat the problems and impediments seriously. Assume the technical people are correct about the problems.

3. Use the rule of three for each potential solution. That is, for each problem, develop three potential reasonable solutions to that problem. That way, everyone understands the problem

well enough. If you only have one potential solution, chances are quite good no one understands the problem well enough to solve it.

4. Involve the communities of practice in generating the solutions to these problems. That's what they are there for. Use them.
5. Ask for project or feature team volunteers to try a solution before committing the program to it. Never impose a solution on the entire program. If no one is willing to volunteer to try a solution, it's not reasonable. Go back to the drawing board.

As the program manager, listen to your teams. If they say, "We can't do this," ask what would enable them to be able to do what you desire. Consider asking them to experiment to become more agile and lean.

Without continuous integration, your program cannot achieve continuous delivery. If you have the possibility to use continuous delivery, what prevents you from doing so? That's an impediment, you as a program manager, can facilitate removing.

7.8 Beware of Technical Debt

The larger and longer your program, the more the teams need to keep the code and tests clean. If they keep the code and tests clean, they can use continuous integration. They can meet all their deliverables to each other. The can collaborate across the organization, because all the code and tests are ready and available for them to work on at any time. If the program encounters a big problem, such as the teams realize the current architecture won't work, the code is in great shape to refactor or redesign.

As a program manager, listen to your teams if they start to say, "We feel pressured to meet a date." My experience (and I bet yours, too) is that when teams try to meet dates, they finesse quality.

In agile, teams finish their work. Limit the feature scope, not quality. That's the way to build a great product in a program.

Eliminate technical debt in each feature. Eliminate technical debt for each iteration or feature set. Eliminate technical debt for each release. If any team needs a hardening sprint, you have technical debt. Find it and eliminate it.

7.9 Invite People to Experiment

One way to assist autonomy, collaboration, and exploration across the program is to invite people to experiment.

An experiment is when you have developed a hypothesis of what is causing a problem or impediment. You decide to try something for some amount of time and measure the results. You need to measure, or you're not experimenting. At the end of that time, you assess the results and decide what to do next.

If you invite people to experiment, or if others invite you to experiment, no one mandates anything for anyone else. No one holds the "secret sauce" for problem solving on the program. That's good, because there is no secret sauce.

The more you invite people to experiment, to create a hypothesis, to try something for a short timebox, to measure the results and decide what to do, the more they take the responsibility for their actions. When they are responsible, they are more likely to succeed.

Some people might not like the word "experiment." Consider these words as alternatives: "trials" or "tinker with the way we work." Regardless of what you call it, work in short timeboxes as teams and measure the results so you can decide what to do next.

Treat people as if they are adults and your equal. (They are equals—they have their parts to do, as do you.) They will respond by acting as if they are adults. If they work across the organization, collaborating in their small-world networks as adults, you will get the results you want—a working product.

7.10 Principles of Encourage Autonomy, Collaboration, and Exploration

1. Autonomy, collaboration, and exploration are the foundation for feature team success. Tell the feature teams that. The principles are: "Continuous attention to technical excellence and good design enhances agility" and "The best architectures, requirements, and designs emerge from self-organizing teams."

2. Encourage small-world networks with email lists and in-person meetings where possible. The principle is: "Amplify learning" and "Face-to-face conversation is the most efficient and effective method of conveying information."

3. Create communities of practice. The principles are: "Continuous attention to technical excellence and good design enhances agility" and "The best architectures, requirements, and designs emerge from self-organizing teams" and "Amplify learning."

CHAPTER 8

Conduct Useful Meetings for Your Program

In the program, people need program-level meetings for several reasons:

- The product owners need to collaborate to update the agile roadmap. See Use Continuous Planning (page 51).
- The product owners need to build MVP backlogs. Product owners might build the backlog first, and ask the team to review the backlog. They might build the backlog alone and present it to the team. It depends on how integrated the product owner is with the team under normal circumstances.
- The software program team needs to solve problems that the feature teams can't solve, and needs to present status reports to the rest of the organization.
- The core team needs to solve problems that the software program team can't solve, and needs to make sure that everyone on the core team is ready for product release.
- The core or the software program team might have a retrospective.
- Either program team might need to provide a status report to the rest of the organization. Each program team might want to have a Big Visible Chart explaining the program state at any time. The program team will need to meet to create that status chart or report.

You have choices for how people conduct these meetings.

8.1 Explaining Status: Do Not Use Standups at the Program Level

You'll notice that none of these meetings are standup meetings. A standup is insufficient for these meetings.

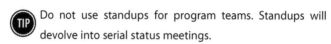 Do not use standups for program teams. Standups will devolve into serial status meetings.

Asking "what did you complete," or even "what did you do since our last standup" is the wrong question. The question is irrelevant because the program team members do not have daily micro-commitments to each other as team members in a feature team do.

That's because the core team members are not a real team in the sense that they don't have interdependent deliverables. Remember, the core team is a group of people whose job is to shepherd the product to release, solving business problems that would prevent release. A standup is also irrelevant for a software program team—too much occurred in the software program if teams are integrating features every day or more often.

If you ask the "since the last standup" question, you create a serial status meeting. Don't do it. Nobody likes serial status meetings. Program teams exist to solve problems and remove obstacles *across the organization*. You, as a program manager may have to report status up, down, and sideways. Do not make your program team members sit through a serial status meeting.

The next question, "What are you working on now" is also irrelevant. You might need to ask about action item/kanban item progress in a part of the meeting, but you don't want to lead with that question.

However, you do need to know what the obstacles are. You also need to know what the interdependencies are. You need to know if deliverables are going to be late. And, the teams need to tell you. That's program management.

You don't learn those issues in a standup. You learn them in other ways.

8.2 Define a Rhythm for Your Program Team

Everyone on the core team or the software program team is busy with their other work. Define a rhythm so these busy people know what to expect for their program commitment and when to expect it. A program cadence shows respect for their time and the other demands of their job.

You don't need to maintain the same cadence throughout the program. You might start with a biweekly (once every two weeks) meeting and transition to a weekly meeting as the product release date gets close.

Some program teams try to work in iterations. Some try to work in kanban.

I recommend using kanban for each program team, so each team can visualize their work in progress.

I also recommend you have weekly or biweekly meetings, depending on the duration of your program. The meetings provide you with a cadence, a rhythm for your work, without having to commit to real iterations.

The problem is that each program team solves different problems, especially if your program is large enough.

The software program team solves technical problems. They answer these questions:

- How can we help the organization understand the progress all the software teams are making as a whole?
- What problems are we encountering as a program?
- How can we as a program team help the teams solve those problems or remove those obstacles?

The last two questions are more tactical approaches to the core team's question, "How can we help the program deliver across the organization?"

The software program team will limit their problem-solving to the software program. If they see problems across the organization that they can't fix, they escalate that problem to the core team.

The core team solves business value problems. They answer these questions:

- How can we help the functions across the organization solve their problems and obtain the information they need?
- What problems are we encountering as a program?
- How can we as a program team help the cross-functional core team solve those problems or remove those obstacles?

The first question addresses the strategy for the program. The last two questions are more tactical approaches to the core team's question, "How can we help the business value of this program?" The core program team will address problems across the organization. If the core team sees problems it can't fix, you, as the core team program manager will have to escalate the problem to your sponsors or management.

How Often Should Your Program Team Meet?

Depending on the projected duration of the program, I have started programs with a biweekly program team meeting. That helps everyone start the program and learn to work together. As the program nears the release date, we move to weekly program team meetings. That's because we have more frequent deliverables. Meet when you need to meet. Not any more often.

The program team is a team in the sense that everyone has the same goal: to release the product. But, almost no one will work *together* on their work. Each person is a delegate from across the organization. The likelihood that the program team can swarm on their problems outside the program team meetings is small. In that sense, the program team is a group.

Maybe you can experiment with your core team meetings. It all depends on how your program is proceeding. I recommend you use a problem-solving meeting agenda. I have suggestions for that agenda in Organize Your Program Team Meetings (page 96).

You can use an action item list, which I used for many years. I now prefer a kanban board, because it shows the number of items in progress. Here is a potential kanban board for a core team:

Ranked Backlog	In Progress		Risk Management or Mitigation	Decision Needed Post-Action	Waiting: Stuck Items	Done
	Action item analysis	Action item resolution				
	Item and date started. Who is working the item.					
MarComm	☐					
Legal				☐	☐	
Sales	☐					
Deployment		☐				
Hardware			☐			

Figure 8.1: Possible Kanban Board for a Core Team

You might prefer an action item list. Make sure you have some chart that exposes the work and especially the work in progress, the WIP.

The program team is a place WIP can hide. Do not let the WIP hide on the program team. You might be close to the end of the program and realize that there are legal agreements to sign, pricing to determine, training to plan, all kinds of things that the core program team needs to deliver. The kanban board for the core team will help that team see their WIP and manage their risks.

How to Manage Long Lead Items

Every so often, you have long lead items. Maybe you have to order equipment. Maybe you have to commit to an outside vendor. Maybe you have to integrate with some other software. You have to commit to something more than three months in advance, well outside of an iteration. You have a long lead item. What do you do?

This is a risk to your program. Manage it as a risk.

Ask yourself, what is the smallest action I can take to see results or action on this long-lead item? How will I know I am getting closer to or farther away from this deliverable? How can you visualize whether you are closer, not farther from this deliverable? Add something every week, an inch-pebble (ROT07), to your kanban, to ensure you make progress on your long-lead items.

8.3 Organize Your Program Team Meetings

Are your program team meetings too large?

"Right Size" Your Program Team Meetings

I once coached a program manager who was attempting to rescue a large program of 16 feature teams. Their program team meetings were a disaster.

Each feature team had a Scrum Master. Each Scrum Master attended the weekly software program team meetings. That program team was not able to make decisions or remove obstacles. The program fell further and further behind, not because they used Scrum, but because they could not agree as a group of 17 people.

The program manager decided to organize the program team meetings first. She said, "You Scrum Masters are all at different levels. Some of you are Scrum of Scrum Masters for several teams working on related feature sets. Some of you have just one feature team working on one feature set. We have a major risk to the program. We are not finishing our program team work because we can't agree on anything. I have a big question: Do you all need to be at this meeting?

"You folks decide. Should you be at this meeting? If not, decide how you will get the information. I will leave it up to you. I work for you." She sat back down and let them work for 30 minutes.

At the end of 20 minutes, they had self-organized into one meeting of four small-program program managers. Each of those program managers had three feature teams working on related feature sets. In addition, there were five independent feature team Scrum Masters. That made nine people plus the program manager and the program product owner.

After the first program team meeting, the independent feature team Scrum Masters decided they didn't need to all be there. One of them came to each meeting, and debriefed the other four later.

The program manager continued to email the agenda to all the Scrum Masters in advance of each meeting, in case they wanted to participate. She sent the minutes to everyone, also, so everyone one felt as if they could see the information.

The program teams had a workable number of people on them, the software program team and the feature program teams. Everyone could make their own decisions and had a way to help information move around the organization.

If you have a large program, look for programs within your program. Find a way to manage the number of people at your program team meetings. See Know Which Program Teams You Need (page 17).

If you still require a delegate from each feature team, create program team norms about how you will make decisions. I have seen these norms work:

- People discuss issues and concerns in advance on a wiki or some other internal project forum.
- If people haven't read the agenda and discussion points in advance, they don't get to participate in a decision.
- If the people who are supposed to be on the program team are also doing technical work, they find someone else to vote as their proxy.
- People agree to use limited consensus so they can experiment and measure, before they reject an idea.

You may need to build team norms for your program team if you have never worked together before. Expect to spend time building team norms at your first program team meeting. Be prepared to iterate on your team norms. You will have to find the norms that work for your team.

8.4 Program Team Meetings Solve Problems

A program manager facilitates an environment for problem solving, a form of servant leadership. It's all about risk management, helping people to be more agile and lean.

1. Consider a problem-solving agenda (page 98) such as the one below.
2. You might decide to have Lean Coffee (page 100) meetings.
3. Consider a Temperature Reading (page 100), especially for retrospectives.

8.4.1 *How to use a problem solving meeting agenda*

I've used and evolved this kind of an agenda over time. Start here and evolve it for your use.

I like to send the agenda in an email to everyone at least 24 hours in advance. In that email, I ask, "Do you have anything for the problem of the week?" If they do respond, I can add it. If not, they might be ready to add it at the time of the meeting checking in.

Include the list of invited participants so everyone knows who is in the meeting or on the call.

Include the location: meeting room or call information, if this is a conference call.

1. Check in with everyone.
2. Visualize the kanban or milestone information. Help people see the short-term and long-term milestones.
3. List the problem(s) of the week. (If you are having biweekly meetings, change this to the problem of the meeting. Or, call it "obstacle removal" or "impediment removal." Use terms that fit for your organization. Remember, the program team exists to solve problems at the program team level, core team level, or software program team level, not at the feature team level.)
   • Discuss each problem. Make sure this is a problem you can solve with this program team. Assess whether you need to timebox the discussion. Decide if you need to split into subteams to discuss the problem and generate solutions. Ask yourselves if you need to escalate the problem if you can't solve it.
   • As a program team, your goal is to resolve each problem by the end of the meeting. But some problems are not 20-minute to one-hour problems. In that case, you need to have a separate meeting to resolve the problem. Put the problem on your kanban board or action item list with a time to resolve it. Don't let this work hide. It's WIP.
4. Review any outstanding action items or kanban items you have not resolved.
5. Adjourn the meeting.

Create a central repository that anyone can access. Use that repository to raise issues and solve problems outside of the meeting. I like meeting notes and action items on a wiki or on their own kanban board.

After the meeting, send the minutes with action items (maybe a picture of the kanban board or a pointer to the board) within 24 hours after the meeting.

8.4.2 How to use lean coffee meetings

When you use lean coffee, everyone brainstorms the list of issues on stickies. You vote on the stickies. You take the highest ranking sticky, discuss that for a short timebox. Consider selecting a timebox of eight minutes and seeing if that works for you. You can always decrease the timebox duration to five minutes, if you like. Do not start with a timebox longer than eight minutes. The idea behind lean coffee is that you discuss something as long as people have energy around it. Longer than eight minutes and the discussion will sag.

At the end of the timebox, you thumb-vote to continue (thumb-up), don't care (thumb-sideways), or change the topic (thumb-down). If you timebox your program team meetings to one hour, you may be surprised by how many issues you can cover in one hour. You might decide to summarize the list of action items or prepare a kanban of the actions at the end of the meeting. If so, either add another 5-10 minutes (timebox this work), or include it in the meeting.

8.4.3 How to use a Temperature Reading

Virginia Satir, a family therapist, developed the temperature reading. You may want to try it for your program team. Alternatively, it's a great way to do retrospectives with a team.

1. Appreciations. An appreciation is a personalized thank you with the reason why. It takes the form of "First Name, I appreciate you for (*something*) because (*for some reason*)."

2. New Information. What new information does anyone have?
3. Puzzles. What puzzles you?
4. Requests for Change. What changes would be helpful?
5. Hopes and Wishes. What hopes and wishes do you have?

8.5 Retrospect at the Program Team Level

Program teams need to reflect and change their approaches just as the feature teams do. They might need to inspect and adapt more often or less often as the teams. Here are some guidelines for when the program team needs to retrospect:

- When the program team has more WIP than they thought was reasonable.
- When people don't finish their deliverables to the program. Deliverables could be training modules from the training department, or legal agreements, or automatic deployment for the software program. These are examples, and the program teams would track them.
- When the program teams don't clear obstacles for anyone in the program.

Aside from a Temperature Reading, consider ways to discover the data and then move into problem solving. Give yourselves enough time—at least a half-day—to understand the issues and develop action items from the retrospective.

If your program team members are geographically distributed, it is even more important to retrospect at regular intervals. The space-time continuum problems may manifest themselves in the feature teams, also. Understand them and solve them.

For more possibilities for retrospectives, see *Agile Retrospectives: Making Good Teams Great*, DER06 and *Getting Value out of Agile Retrospectives: A Toolbox of Retrospective Exercises*, GLI15.

8.6 Principles for Conduct Useful Meetings for Your Program

1. Define the purpose for your meetings. Make sure you have the people you need. Timebox the meetings, if necessary, so people don't spend all day at the meetings. The principles are: "Eliminate waste" and "Business people and developers must work together."

2. Don't have meetings you don't need to have. The principle is: "Eliminate waste."

3. Create a public online forum so everyone can see the discussions your program team is having. This will help the transparency of your program, and help people see you are working on removing obstacles. The principles are: "Amplify learning" and "Business people and developers must work together."

CHAPTER 9

Estimating Program Schedule or Cost

If you have ever used waterfall approaches to programs, you and the teams spent a fair amount of time estimating how long the program would take or how much it would cost. Now, even if you are using agile, your managers might want to know, "How long will this program take?" Or, they will want to know, "How much will this beast cost?"

Your managers asked for estimates, because back in the waterfall days, estimates were the one way they could manage the program risk. In waterfall, we were supposed to update the estimate at the end of each phase. We don't have phases in agile, so your managers might not realize they have other ways to manage program risk at an operations review meeting or a project portfolio management meeting.

However, you have other levers at your disposal to manage program risk and report status. See Useful Measurements in an Agile and Lean Program (page 177).

The best lever you have to manage risk is the fact that you can see working product all the time. If you use the idea of internal releases at least each month, your managers don't need to ask for estimates.

Managers today may ask for estimates because they think they can add more people to your program and reduce the necessary time. They are mistaken.

Once you have one feature team per feature set backlog, you may not need any more teams on your program. You can ask feature teams, "Would it be useful to work in conjunction with another team to reduce the time?" Listen to what the feature teams say.

Adding more people or more teams to your program may slow it down, especially if the program is late. Adding more people or teams increases the communication overhead. If the program is late, you will encounter Brooks' Law from *The Mythical Man-Month* (BRO95).

Help your managers see that they have levers other than the estimate for your program. In an agile or lean organization, as long as the feature teams complete a feature every day or so, the managers can say, "Stop" whenever the program has enough working. Spending time estimating instead of delivering makes little sense for an agile program.

9.1 Does Your Organization Want Resilience or Prediction?

If your management is new to agile, they may not realize that agile and lean provides the program resilience. Estimation is prediction, and your teams can estimate work that is close and small with good results. However, the larger or farther off the work is, the worse the estimate is likely to be.

Once the teams start delivering, you can explain the value of resilience—the ability to change fast.

Ask your management what they want: resilience or prediction? If they say prediction, maybe they will change their minds after the teams produce working product and continue producing more working product.

If they say resilience, they trust the product owner value team to rank the features. The managers also trust the teams to complete features. Work with your managers to build trust so they don't need as many estimates as they used to.

9.2 Ask These Questions Before Estimating

If your managers still want to know how much the program will cost or how long it will take, remind them that these questions are the wrong questions. You, as the program manager can ask,

- How much would you like to invest in time, money, or learning before we stop?
- Are you ready to watch the program grow as we build it so you can stop us when you don't want to invest anymore?
- What is the value of this project or program to you?

It's much easier to manage investment than it is to predict an estimate. With an agile roadmap, your sponsors can help select the investment direction, too.

It's easy to answer the "How much would you like to invest" question, as long as the program always has demonstrable or releasable product. Either your sponsors will say, "I've seen enough. Please stop." Or, they will say, "I like what I see. Please keep going." Or, they might say, "I sort of like what I see, and I'd like you to change this and that, please."

It's easy to work with people like that. It's much more difficult to estimate a whole program.

But, what if your sponsors need some kind of a ballpark estimate, something that gives them an idea of how much or how long this program will last? You may need a gross estimate because your sponsors may want to limit their time and money investment. They may want to stop before reaching NRE, Non-Recurring Engineering expenses.

Here are some ideas.

9.3 Targets Beat Estimates

Working toward a target, either date or budget, is much easier than trying to estimate a large program.

If your sponsors say, "Here is your target date," or "Don't exceed this budget," that's great. You can manage the program risks to meet that target date or budget. You can work towards a target, making sure you have, at minimum, monthly deliverables that are releasable product.

You will have to help the product owners focus on the most valuable roadmap. You will have to watch the run rate for the program. You will have to work with the feature teams to make sure they produce monthly demonstrations or working product.

9.4 Generate an Estimate with a Percentage Confidence

If you must estimate, try a gross estimate with a percentage confidence.

Your estimate will be wrong, but if you call it a "Gross Estimate with a Percentage Confidence," a "Prediction," or a "Forecast," you are more likely to get the result you want.

Remind your sponsors that estimates are guesses, not promises.

Assuming you have teams and they have some idea of what is in their feature sets or backlogs, try this approach:

9.4.1 Option 1: Teams estimate their own ranked backlogs

For a program, each team does this for its own ranked backlog:

- Take every item on the backlog and roadmap, and use whatever relative sizing approach you use now to estimate. If you have small features, you can count them. Remember, because you are agile, you may not do the work farther out on the roadmap. You have uncertainty, not just in sizing, but in whether you will implement those features.

- Walk through the entire backlog, estimating as you proceed. Don't worry about how large the features are. Keep a *count* of the large features. Decide as a team if this feature is larger than two or three team-days. If it is, keep a count of those features. The larger the features, the more uncertainty you have in your estimate.

- As a team, add all your relative estimates for your features. Add up the number of large features. Now, you have a relative estimate which, based on your previous velocity, means something to you. You also have a number of large features, which will decrease the confidence in that estimate.

- Do you have 50 features, of which only five are large? Maybe you have 75% confidence in your estimate. On the other hand, maybe all of your features are large. I might only have 5-10% confidence in the estimate. Why? Because the team hasn't completed any work yet and you have no idea how long your work will take.

Team	Relative Estimate
Team 1	12 weeks duration, 50% confidence
Team 2	16 weeks duration, 25% confidence
Team 3	8 weeks duration, 90% confidence
Team 4	10 weeks duration, 10 % confidence
Team 5	7 weeks duration, 90% confidence

Figure 9.1: Program Team Estimates by Team

Here's what this might look like on a program. Assume you have five teams, each with its own ranked backlog. Each team assesses their backlog and turns it into an estimate with a percentage confidence level. In this example, you have teams with confidence levels ranging from 10% to 90%. That says the backlog items are not small enough for the teams to estimate a reasonable size. Or, that there is so much risk that the teams can't provide you a more precise estimate.

You might want to know, "When will this program be done?" but you can't know it without the teams doing some work.

As a software program team, get together, and assess the total estimate. Does the software program team need to add time for any current obstacles? If so, add time and increase the percentage uncertainty.

Once the software program team has some kind of an estimate, the software program manager can bring that estimate to the core program team.

In parallel to the software program estimation, the core team needs to generate their estimates for their plans. Once everyone has estimates, the core team can assess how long they will take as a core team. And, the software program manager can present the software program estimate.

Now, the core team can review the entire estimate and generate a number for the people who asked for an estimate.

9.4.2 Option 2: Ask experts to estimate on behalf of the teams

If you have a roadmap, but have not assigned feature teams yet, consider asking experts in the organization. They will have estimation bias. You don't know how much estimation bias they have.

Ask the experts to estimate on behalf of the teams, using the same percentage confidence approach above. When you report the number to management, explain that you do not know how much estimation bias there is in the estimate. Your sponsors would be better off letting the teams work for a couple of weeks and seeing results. They could then answer the questions:

- How much would you like to invest before we stop?
- What is the value of this project or program to you?"

An estimate from experts may not even be an order of magnitude correct.

9.4.3 Option 3: You estimate on behalf of the entire program

When my managers have asked me for a program estimate, I ask them if they have a target date in mind. I remind them that we are working incrementally, and we can change. I remind them that I am a program manager, and have no ability to see into the future. I remind them that I can help the teams produce working product often. But, asking me for a date is not going to make that occur faster.

If you say something like this nicely—and it depends on your culture as to how you say it—you may be able to understand what your sponsors or managers do want. If your organization is new to agile, your managers might not realize that the product owners are in charge of when a feature is scheduled in the backlog.

Never allow a target date to compromise the quality of your program. Maintaining technical excellence allows the teams to maintain their sustainable pace and keep releasing, internally and externally.

Both options 2 and 3 have problems. If anyone estimates on behalf of the teams, the teams may have no interest in committing to that estimate. Why would they?

All too often, managers use the estimates that other people create as a target or "incentive" for the feature teams. That is a terrible way to use these estimates. The teams have no control over their work. Can the teams sustain their pace to meet these estimates? Can the teams work as self-organizing teams to deliver?

When someone else provides teams with a target, and then tries to force a commitment to that target, you know that Murphy's Law is going to sit on your program and make it impossible for the teams to deliver working features in the desired time. Don't do it.

9.5 Present Your Estimate as a Prediction

I assume you have experienced agile teams. If not, the teams have probably padded their estimates. Either that, or the features are large epics or themes, and the uncertainty is high.

The more experienced the teams are at agile, the better the estimate is. The more the teams are feature teams, the better the estimate is because the teams know how to work and learn together. If you are new to agile, or have a mixed program (agile and non-agile teams), you know that the estimate will be way off.

The software program manager can say, "We have an initial order-of-magnitude prediction. But we haven't tested this prediction with any work, so we don't know how accurate our estimates are. Right now our confidence is about 5-10% (or whatever it is) in our prediction. We've spent a day or so estimating, because we would rather spend time delivering, instead of estimating. We need to do a week or two of work, deliver a working skeleton, and then we can tell you more about our prediction. We can better our prediction as we proceed. Remember, back in the waterfall days, we spent a month estimating and we were wrong. This way, you'll get to see product as we work."

Use the word "prediction" as much as possible, because people understand the word prediction. They hear weather predictions all the time. They know about weather predictions. But when they hear estimates of work, they think you are correct, even if you use confidence numbers, they think you are accurate. Use the word prediction.

Consider setting your management's expectations by saying, "Here is a prediction for our first milestone (internal release). We can provide a much better estimate for the next milestone." Incremental estimation works as well as incremental budgeting does.

9.6 Spiral in on an Estimate

Spiraling in on a date works quite well for smaller, shorter programs. I have used this approach for four-to-eight month programs. I offer

"Quarter 2, next year," as my first estimate. As we finish features and have internal releases, I update the estimate to "February-March." As we finish work and I can see how we deliver, I can say, "The first couple of weeks in March, sometime."

As we finish more work, I can work with the program product owner to see if we still have remaining value in the roadmap and if we need to ask teams to work outside their normal deliverables to make that date.

9.7 Supply a Three-Date Estimate

With a three-date estimate, you offer your managers this information:

- The earliest possible date the teams might complete the program. This is the optimistic date.
- A more likely date the teams might complete. This is the realistic date.
- A date by which you are sure the teams can complete the program. This is the pessimistic date.

Never supply just one date with your estimate. That one date invites your management to play estimation games with you. When you supply a three-date estimate, you invite them to understand your risks.

The longer the program, the farther out your realistic and pessimistic dates should be. When I have used this, I have said, "We should have a demonstrable overall product by June 1, but I don't think we can release that one to our customers. We should have a reasonable delivery date of August 15. If Murphy comes to sit on our program, don't expect a releasable product until October 30. And, I should be able to update this estimate next month, when we can all see what the teams deliver."

I have found that if I set my managers' expectations about what they can expect to see, they understand this kind of estimation.

9.8 **Do You Really Need an Estimate?**

I have worked on many programs in my professional life. My managers gave me targets for demonstrations, trade shows, and when the program had to deliver. Sometimes, my managers gave me a "not to exceed" budget. I have never been asked the "How much" question. That's because the program delivered monthly demonstrations or releases. Management could see our progress.

When it comes to delivering products, if you provide interim value, the "How much" question goes away. Your management trusts the program to continue delivering value.

Deliver internal releases. Show a walking skeleton and then keep building small features. Keep ranking backlog items by value. Keep asking the "How much do you want to invest?" question.

You won't have to estimate the entire program.

9.9 **Beware of These Program Estimation Traps**

There are plenty of potential traps when you estimate programs. Here are some common problems:

- The backlog is full of themes. You haven't even gotten to epics, never mind stories. No one can make a useful prediction. That's like my saying, "I can go from Boston to China on an airplane. It will take time." I need more data: which time of year? Midweek, weekend? Otherwise, I can only provide a ballpark, not a real estimate. Any estimate anyone provides will be off by orders of magnitude, and you don't know how many. The teams will have to spend time breaking the themes into feature sets, time they could spend developing working product.
- Worse, the backlog is full of tasks, so you don't know the value of a story. "Fix the radio button" does not explain the value of a story. Maybe we can eliminate the button instead of fixing it. You don't know if you have a valuable working product at the end of all the tasks.

- The people estimating are not the ones who will do the work, so the estimate is full of estimation bias. Just because work looks easy or looks hard does not mean it is. If your senior managers believe this estimate, they will feel disappointed and frustrated when the teams take more time than the estimators expected.
- The estimate becomes a target. This never works, but managers do it all the time. "You estimated it would take a quarter to do this work. Prove it!" Some managers do not understand that an estimate is a prediction or a guess.
- The people on your program multitask, so the estimate is wrong. See *Predicting the Unpredictable: Pragmatic Approaches to Estimating Cost or Schedule*, (ROT15) for more information.
- Managers think they can predict team size from the estimate. This is the problem of splitting work in the mistaken belief that more people make it easier to do more work. More people make the communications burden heavier.

Estimating a program is more difficult, because you somehow have to add disparate estimates with different percentage confidences. A better way to manage the issues of a program is to decide if the program is worth funding (by value) in the project portfolio. Then, work in an agile way. Be ready to change the order of work in the backlog, for teams and among teams.

As a program manager, you have two roles when people ask for estimates: check with your sponsors and request the teams deliver often. Ask your sponsors the questions in Ask these questions before estimating (page 104).

Explain to the teams and product owners the results the organization needs:

- A walking skeleton (of features in the product) and build on it.
- Small features, so we can see the product evolve every day.

The more the sponsors see the product take shape, the less interested they will be in an overall estimate. They may ask for more specific estimates (when can you do this specific feature), which is much easier to answer.

Delivering working software builds trust. Trust obviates many needs for estimates. If your managers or customers have never had trust with a project or program team before, they will start asking for estimates. Your job is to deliver working software every day, so they stop asking.

9.10 Estimation Do's and Don'ts for Program Managers

There are several do's and don'ts for estimation. Here are some common problems:

9.10.1 Estimation don'ts:

- Never provide a single point estimate. If you provide a single point estimate of either a date or money, people will expect that specific date or that much money. Even if you are just 10% over, they will think you have failed. I am serious.

- Estimating by anyone on behalf of the teams. If anyone estimates for the teams, they have no reason to meet that estimate. Why would they? Would you?

- Trying to enforce overtime to meet an estimate. Agile is built on the idea of sustainable pace. Disregard that at your peril. You will create technical debt, lose collaboration, and defeat the idea of autonomy and exploration.

- Never let managers try to add relative estimates from teams together. That's like trying to add oranges from one team and frogs from another team. You want teams to work at their own velocity or cycle time. As long as they can create features from a backlog, you don't care what they call their relative estimation.

9.10.2 Estimation do's:

- Listen to the teams. Once they provide you with their estimates, thank them and use their estimates.
- Plan to iterate. This is agile. The backlogs will change, which means the estimates will change. It's your job as the program manager to explain that to your sponsors.
- Estimates expire. If your sponsors think that an estimate is good for all time, disabuse them of that notion. Every estimate has an expiration date. Help your sponsors see that instead of estimates, they want to see working product.

For more details on estimates and what works and doesn't work, see *Predicting the Unpredictable: Pragmatic Approaches to Estimating Cost or Schedule*, ROT15.

9.11 Principles of Estimating Schedule or Cost

1. Never add relative estimates together or compare team estimates. Every team works at a different pace. Each team's velocity is personal. The principles are: "Working software is the primary measure of progress" and "Simplicity."

2. Use a percentage confidence, so everyone understands that, especially at the beginning of the program, you have no idea how long the program will take. The principle is: "Business people and developers must work together."

3. Working product is better than estimation. Build working product fast. See if working product will take the place of estimates for your management. If necessary, work toward a target date or budget. The principle is: "Working software is the primary measure of progress."

CHAPTER 10

Useful Measurements in an Agile and Lean Program

Part of what you might need to do in your program team meetings is to prepare your program's status for the rest of the organization. You might have some sort of Operations Review meeting. Because the organization expects some progress on your program, you might need to show progress to the people who make project portfolio decisions.

Use the information in this chapter to work with your sponsors and learn what your management requires and how you need to show your management progress. Working software is the best measure of progress.

When your program delivers working product frequently, you build trust with the people who want estimates or measurements. You might need to review How Often Can You Release Your Product? (page 71).

You may still have to provide a run rate, or some other financial report to those folks. On the other hand, they won't worry about whether your program is worth the money they have invested—they can see the results when they see working product.

Working product builds trust in a way that any measurement does not. That may be the best status report you can provide.

You want measurements that mean something useful at the program level. Consider how you might explain to anyone about what the program has completed and what remains not yet done.

As always, the best measurement is working product. However, that is not the only measurement you can take that means something at the program level.

Working product should be your primary measurement. It is how you will see progress.

10.1 What Measurements Will Mean Something to Your Program?

Measurements come in two flavors: predictive indicators and lagging indicators. Of course, you want predictive indicators. You have a large effort.

What do you have for a one-team agile project? You have velocity, burnup charts, and cumulative flow. Can you use these measures at the program level?

You cannot use velocity at the program level. It is not a predictive measure. Here's why.

10.2 Never Use Team-Based Measurements for a Program

I see a ton of measurement dysfunction when it comes to large programs. Measurement is one place where if you try to say, "Here's what each team does. What does this mean for the program?" you will get into trouble.

Do not even think about taking project team measurements and adding them together. That's like taking my husband's weight and mine, adding them together, dividing by two and determining our average jean size. It makes just as much sense to try to determine "average" velocity or cumulative flow or average anything when you do that with teams.

Any team-based measurement is for that team to use as their guide.

10.2.1 Do Not Use Velocity As a Program Measure

Velocity is a team-based measurement. Teams can use velocity as a diagnostic tool to see how they are doing. Velocity is not a good program-level measurement.

One of the mistakes I see a lot is that managers want to take several teams' velocity and somehow add them together. They think this a program measure of velocity.

Don't do that. Velocity is personal to one team. It's only predictive to that team and it's only predictive for estimation purposes. It's not predictive to any other team. You can see what teams are doing if they are feature teams, and you use a product backlog burnup chart.

You can't use velocity to predict *program* progress either. Why? Because as the product owners get better at making the stories smaller—and you want them to become better at this—the number of stories may well increase per iteration. That will change a team's velocity.

But, what if you are a program manager or a product owner and you see a team that used to produce running, tested features at a regular clip suddenly slow down? What do you do?

The first question is this: Does it matter? Maybe this team is helping another team. Maybe they are so far ahead on their feature set that it doesn't matter. Do you know?

Second, are you the right person to interfere? Is there someone else, a project manager, a product owner, a coach, or a Scrum Master who might lead a retrospective and ask these questions? If you are the correct person, here are some questions you might ask:

- Has the team encountered any obstacles recently that have affected their ability to produce running, tested features? (You can remove obstacles.)
- Is anyone on the team multitasking? (Make sure this team is dedicated to your program. That is an obstacle you can address.)
- Has the team reviewed their velocity charts or cycle time to see what's going on? A velocity chart or cycle time chart can help a team solve their problems. (The team might not realize what's happening. Once they know, the team can address this concern.)
- Does the team need any help from you?

Expect the team to be able to identify its problems. If a team knows it has a problem and can't identify it, they can ask you for help. I've seen agile teams who worked well as independent teams have trouble integrating into a program. So far, all those teams I've seen have identified their problems and needed help solving them.

You can add value by suggesting ways they can find help or by acquiring the help they need.

10.3 Measure by Features, Not by Teams

So, we have team measurements that don't add up. What can we use? Feature-based measurements.

Programs are all about features. That means you measure by feature. Sometimes, multiple teams work off the same shared backlog. Does it matter if you measure what a team does? It matters for the team. It does not matter for the program.

But, the program manager cares about the program's progress on features across the teams. If the entire program has lurching progress, as in teams that are not integrating something each day, that's a problem. It means that you might have all or some of these problems: too many features in progress, no continuous integration, and/or the work-in-progress in the teams is too high.

So, how do you measure this? You could measure "Number of features completed per iteration." Why not story points? Because customers don't buy story points. Customers buy features. They only buy running tested features. That's it.

This is where the program bumps up against the project portfolio.

Now, it happens that each feature is some number of story points. And, the way to make more features is to break them down into smaller slices. Yes, this is gaming the system. All measurements can be gamed. All of them. However, especially in a large effort such as a program, you want small features. You will see progress faster with minimum marketable features. So, it's okay if your product owners start making smaller features.

One way to make smaller features is to do what Pawel Brodzinski says in *Minimum Indispensable Feature Set*, (BRO14):

"The reason is that most of the time I can instantly come with the batch of work that is one third, one fifth or one tenth of what was labelled an Minimal Viable Product by a potential client and it would still validate a business hypothesis behind a product. It likely means that with a bit of effort and better understanding of the context our clients would be able to cut it down way further than that. It may mean that they'd be even able to validate the basic idea without writing any software at all." —Pawel Brodzinski

Note that his Minimal Indispensable Feature Set is very small.

When you start measuring by features, you can create small wins. When the program can release more often, your program builds trust.

10.4 Measure Completed Features

If you have an agile roadmap, you can measure the number of features done and the number of features remaining to complete, against the total number of features. This provides everyone with a chance to see when the features increase, and the progress made against the roadmap. The smaller the features on the roadmap, the better this chart will be.

Allow for the increase of features because creating software is about learning. As the teams finish features, they and their product owners will realize they need to do something else. That's fine. Allow for it.

Figure 10.1 on page 122, the Program Feature Chart shows that things change in a program.

The roadmap will change. That means the backlogs for the teams will change. Make that visible to everyone. Otherwise, everyone wants to know, "Why can't you predict this program's cost?" Allow for change and help other people understand the changes.

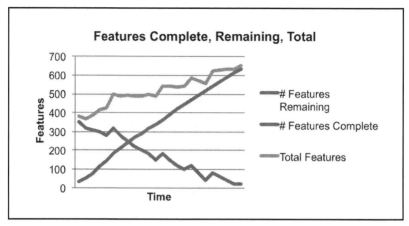

Figure 10.1: Program Feature Chart

With this kind of a chart, you can discuss the inevitable changes. And, when people ask you, "How much will this program cost," you can ask them, "When would you like us to re-estimate the product backlog?"

If your programs are anything like the programs I've worked on, they fall into a couple of categories: the first is the kind we have to do, because they are critical to the organization's success. The big question is when we will release the darn thing, so we will adjust the roadmap and the backlog. The second is when we want to release the darn thing as quickly as possible because we need the money, darn it, so we have to play with the roadmap and the backlog to get the most value out of what we're doing. (Do you have a third?)

Did you notice the common theme here: we will have to play with the roadmap and the backlog to get the most value out of the program? Notice I did not say ROI (return on investment). You cannot calculate ROI until after you release, so there's no point in trying to measure that right now.

Your management might want you to measure Earned Value. Earned Value is the value you derive from completed features. With earned value, your management might be able to capitalize the investment the program has made. You can show earned value with a product backlog burnup chart.

10.5 Measure the Product Backlog Burnup

The next chart is the product backlog burnup chart. This is where you take all the feature sets, plot them next to each other on one chart and show how they might be done in relationship to each other.

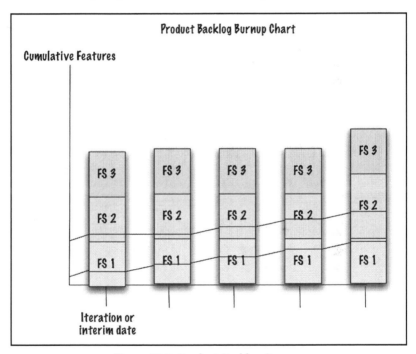

Figure 10.2: Product Backlog Burnup

This product backlog burnup chart is what we might have had for a product I worked on long ago, a voicemail system.

Each part of the system has a different feature team working on it. We had different teams for each part of the system: Alarms, Messages, Payments, Ringback, User Admin, and CO Admin. We had more teams, but this is a simplified version of the chart. After the teams worked on the code for five interim releases, this is what the chart looked like:

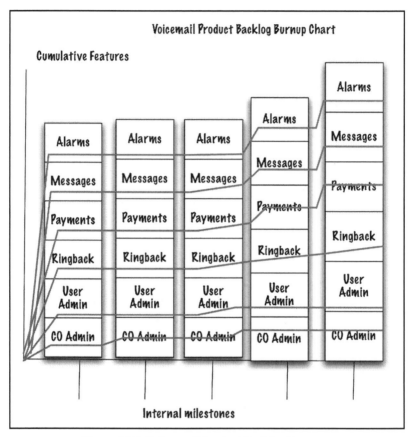

**Figure 10.3: Voicemail Product Backlog Burnup,
After Several Interim Releases**

The number of features increased over time for all of the feature sets. Management was surprised when they saw the requirements growth. The product backlog burnup chart, shows feature growth with the height of each feature set in the chart.

In a sense, this is a thermometer kind of chart for each feature set. You can see the completion of each feature set grow as the teams deliver code into the code base.

10.6 Measure the Time to Your Releasable Deliverable

Since what you care about is releasable product at the program level, measure the time to achieve it. Measure the time between releasable deliverables. Does the product go from releasable to not releasable?

This is a predictive indicator, believe it or not. Because you are accustomed to releasing on a rhythm, your past time-to-release is a predictor of your future time-to-release. Unless you know how to shorten that time, it's not going to become shorter without significant effort. You can't get feedback in less time than your time to release. This is important to the program.

If you release internally every month, and that release is good enough to ship, then your time to release is 30 days.

If you have continuous delivery, you might measure your time to release in hours or minutes. If you do have a SaaS product, and you are not releasing in hours or minutes, you may have an impediment in your program. You, as the program manager, may need to help solve that problem.

If your programs takes longer than 30 days to release, why? That might be an impediment for your program. The longer it takes for you to release, the long it takes for feedback to the product development teams.

The larger your program, the more feedback you need. Measure it.

10.7 Measure Release Frequency

If your program starts releasing something internally every two weeks, and some time later the program releases only once each three weeks, something bad has happened. The teams might have incurred technical debt without anyone realizing it.

If your program starts releasing five times a day and builds up to releasing every 20 minutes, you might not have problems in the program.

Your release frequency is an indication of how easy it is to release your product. You want internal release frequency high, regardless of your ability to externally release.

10.8 Measure Build Time

One indication that your program is healthy is the amount of time it takes to do a full build or a partial build. The lower the build time, the more frequently the developers will check in and build. The more frequently people check in and build, the more likely they are to do continuous integration. You can maintain momentum on your program.

Be aware when build times increase. Or, if performance is a key feature of your product, be aware if certain scenarios have decreased performance or reliability. If you—and the feature teams—are aware of the build time and performance scenarios, everyone can know if something breaks.

Measure build time as a trend. The teams might want to measure broken builds and time to fix a build as trends, also. Build time measurements are an indication that the code is healthy or not.

10.9 Other Potential Measurements

You may need to take and provide other measurements for your sponsors, or for your program team.

10.9.1 Measure run rate if you have a target budget

If you have a target budget, measure the run rate. The run rate is the amount of salary and overhead the program uses every week or iteration or every month.

A cautionary note here: Do not ask people to track their time by feature. It is rarely accurate.

If the *teams* find value in that total team-time per feature, they can measure it. They might measure it to see if they can make their features smaller so they can obtain more throughput. As a program manager, I am interested in the aggregate number of how much we spend per week or month, so I know where we are in relation to the target budget. That's the run rate.

That also provides you the excuse to ask everybody, "You're not working on any other project or program, are you? Because I'm taking your salary hit on this program. So if you're working on something else, let me know!"

Multitasking is a disaster on a program. It's insidious and slows a program to a crawl faster than anything I know.

10.9.2 Consider cumulative flow, to see work in progress

Depending on the number of teams, you might be able to look at cumulative flow or work in progress. The more teams you have, the more this entire graph can get too large to be effective.

Each team can consider measuring its cumulative flow, to make sure they don't have work in progress or inventory.

10.9.3 Consider a program-level obstacle report

You might track an obstacle report, as I suggest in *Manage Your Project Portfolio*, ROT09.

Your feature teams want to know you are looking for and removing obstacles. They are impediments to your program. The program teams

Obstacle Report			
Rank	Obstacle	Request Date	Days Since Request Date
1	Chair for Jim	Feb 1	15
2	Need tester full time	Jan 1	44
3	Standup meeting area with whiteboard	Jan 7	38

Figure 10.4: Program Obstacle Report

want to know, also. As a program manager, your primary job is to facilitate the teams finishing their work. When feature teams see the program team's progress removing obstacles, they can see and feel your progress. That progress encourages them to bring you bad news and trust you to remove obstacles.

When you make the obstacle report public, no managers can hide from their obstacle-removal work. The managers have to commit to helping the program.

10.9.4 *Consider other measures as diagnostic indicators*

If your program feels stuck, you might want the teams to measure their Fault Feedback Ratios as in *Manage It! Your Guide to Modern, Pragmatic Project Management*, (ROT07).

You might want to measure code growth over time. If your feature teams don't have small growth, that might be a problem. This is a team data point. You can measure code growth for the entire code base. You would want to see where the code growth is larger than expected to do some problem-solving—not blaming! People grow code fast when they are under pressure. Learn why people are—or feel as if they are—under pressure. Do not blame them for being under pressure.

If you see a high fault feedback ratio, look for bad news. Consider more options in How Servant Leaders Work (page 135).

You might want to track defects/feature, although if you have many, I suggest doing something about that sooner rather than later. Your technical debt will get out of control very fast, and reduce your momentum. Remember that incurring technical debt has a cost. If left unchecked, technical debt will prevent the teams from releasing because the features are not actually done.

10.10 Measure Performance or Reliability Release Criteria

I have worked on products where they existed because they provided a performance or reliability advantage over their competitors. One way to monitor that advantage is to build the measurements into the release criteria. Then, create product measurements that allow you to monitor the competitive advantage with each build.

"We Learned to Measure Performance"

I was the program manager for a database product. We sold it based on performance.

I had the bright idea we should measure performance with an interim release, about halfway through the program.

The performance had degraded so we were much worse than our competitors. I didn't ask why—I figured the developers and architects would do that. But I did ask for each team to generate automated performance tests we could run against every build. We knew what the performance needed to be. If the performance was too slow, we could fix it then, not accumulate technical debt.

That worked. We ended up with eight scenarios. We had a pre-loaded database, so we could run the tests fast. We ran them and discovered problems as we proceeded.

I wasn't so worried about the problems. I was worried about our not knowing about the problems until very late in the program.

Having performance scenarios and running automated tests every build that represented those scenarios saved our collective tushes.

—A Senior Program Manager

10.11 How to Answer the "When Will You Be Done/How Much Will Your Program Cost" Question

If your management constantly asks you for estimation, they don't trust you or the program. A request for estimation is also a measurement. It's a qualitative measurement of your influence on the managers and the teams. It's a measure of how much your management trusts you. Better you should know now, when you can do something about it.

Back in Ask these questions before estimating (page 104), I suggested you ask your sponsors about investment or value.

You can see that with the approaches I've suggested, the program always has something to show your sponsors. You always have a walking skeleton. You always either had a demonstration within the last two weeks, or you have one coming up. If you have an agile roadmap the way I suggest, you even have at least a monthly release, or a demo. You have a program product owner who continues to work on the roadmap.

Armed with the roadmap and historical data about what the teams have delivered, and the product backlog burnup chart, you can ask the people who ask, "When will your program be done?" this question, "What is of most value to you? Once we know what is of most value, we can work on that first. If the backlog is already ranked in value order, we can either take the time to estimate it, or I can provide an estimate with a confidence level in a couple of days."

It's the same kind of answer with the cost question. The only problem is if these people ask before you've started anything at all. That's really a project portfolio question.

If your sponsors want your program to continue estimating either schedule or budget after you have started to show them a deliverable each month, ask why.

- Is your program's demonstration a feature-based demonstration or a frameworks demo? Sponsors and customers don't buy frameworks. The teams need to deliver features.

- Can your sponsors see progress based on your program's demo, or are the teams developing as components, instead of through the architecture? Sponsors and customers cannot see the value of components. They need to see features.
- Is there a target date or a target budget you need to know about? If so, you can manage to that risk.

If your sponsors want your program to spend time estimating instead of delivering, you can do that. In the past, I have explained that all the time we spend estimating is time we don't spend delivering. If you have agile or lean teams delivering features all the time, your sponsors will understand.

10.12 **Principles**

1. Measure at the program level, not at the project level. The principle is: "Build integrity in."
2. Measure what you want to see. You want completed features. You want releasable code. What else do you want? Measure that. Do not measure surrogates. The more you measure surrogates, the less you will get what you want. The principle is: "Working software is the primary measure of progress."
3. The feature teams are also responsible for their measurements. They need to measure what they do to know if they are going off the rails and if they have risks in their projects. The principle is: "Build projects around motivated individuals. Trust them to get the job done."
4. Ask for demonstrations. Remember in the manifesto, on the principles page, there is a line that says, "Working software is the primary measure of progress." Believe it. The more your product works, the fewer measurements you need. The principle is: "Working software is the primary measure of progress."

CHAPTER 11

Develop Your Servant Leadership

The senior people in agile and lean programs are servant leaders. The program product owner, the program managers, the program architect are all servant leaders. They guide and shepherd the business value of the program. They create the environment in which all teams and team members can contribute to the product.

If you are unsure of what a servant leader is or how it changes how you work, this is the chapter for you.

Servant leadership is an approach to managing and leading where the leader creates an environment in which people can do their best work. The leader doesn't control the work; the team does. The leader trusts the team to provide the desired results.

Servant leaders put the needs of customers, employees, and communities first. This allows you to create an environment in which people come first. That creates business value when you ask for the results you want.

11.1 Program Managers No Longer "Drive" the Program

Some program managers have used the position to bully people into working "faster." Or, to demand that teams complete some functionality by working overtime. Or, they would commit to a date or functionality without the teams' knowing whether the work could be done, never mind in that time. One of my program managers once told a customer, "Sure, they can do that." We would have had to bend the laws of physics at the time. Our computers were too slow then.

When organizations transition to agile, the program manager might want to work as a servant leader. However, the management might want to be command-and-control. Or, at least control. You might find it difficult to work as a servant leader in this situation. That makes it difficult to be a servant leader to the program and manage the managers' expectations.

11.2 Consider Your Servant Leadership

In reality, you may work on a continuum from servant leadership to command and control leadership.

I had a program product owner who was "too busy" to spend time iterating on the roadmaps for our program. I pinged him several times to update the roadmap. I explained the program was at risk. He had other work that appeared more important to him.

I was concerned we would have no backlogs for the next month and no updated roadmap. I made an appointment for a one-on-one with him. We had a cordial conversation. No action on the roadmap.

I saw him the next week and said, "You have two days to update the roadmap. If you don't, I'll get someone who will. You'll be off the program."

He laughed at me. "I'll do it when I get around to it."

I said, "Don't tempt me. Two days."

The two days came and went. I made an appointment with his boss and explained he was no longer on my program. Did the boss want to assign someone new, or could I have my pick of potential program product owners?

His boss wanted me to give the guy a second chance. No, no way.

I got my new program product owner. We had an updated roadmap and a new backlog.

You might think I was not so serving in this instance. I didn't yell or swear. I admit to some eye-rolling. I served the greater needs of the program.

Being a servant leader does not mean you are a pushover. It means you create the environment in which people can thrive and the feature teams can work with autonomy, collaboration, and exploration. If people don't know what to do, they certainly cannot deliver.

11.3 How Servant Leaders Work

In *The Case for Servant Leadership*, KEI08, Kent Keith defines seven practices of servant leaders:

1. They are self-aware.
2. They listen.
3. They serve the people who work "for" them. (Keith calls this "Changing the Pyramid.")
4. They help other people grow.
5. They coach people, not control them.
6. They unleash the energy and intelligence of others.
7. They work to develop their foresight, so they can act, not react.

Program servant leaders act as stewards of the program environment. They might protect the teams from interference. They facilitate the teams' work. For more information on servant leadership, see *A Journey into the Nature of Legitimate Power and Greatness, 25th Anniversary Edition*, GRE02.

When you ask the teams for the results you want, when you create the environment in which the teams can deliver those results, and when you manage by exception, you are a servant leader.

Here's how you might use these practices.

Our managers ask us to be program managers, program architects, or program product owners because we have shown our expertise or competence in the past. When we are self-aware, we don't need to be the "smartest" or the best technical person. Instead, we are aware of our strengths and how we can manage our weaknesses.

When we listen and decide that our job is to serve the people in the program, what matters is how people can finish their work. It matters that everyone has the capability to do their jobs—that we listen for and remove impediments.

We may be the technical leader for some part of the program. Program architects often discover they are technical leaders. One of the most valuable actions for a servant leader is to help other people use our expertise to improve the product or the program. When we coach people instead of specifying their work, we help them learn and grow.

When we deliberate about how to create an environment in which people can be most successful, we have two opportunities. The first is that we unleash everyone else's capabilities. They can be even more successful. The other is that we have the opportunity to see the program as a whole and act before risks become problems.

11.4 Some People Don't Want Servant Leadership

When I coach managers and architects to improve their servant leadership, some people say, "But, some people want me to tell them what to do. They don't want a servant leader. They want a commanding leader."

If you hear that, review your program and corporate culture. Are your managers telling you how to work? If so, you might feel as if you need to tell others how to do their work. Do your managers blame you for making mistakes? If so, do you blame the people on the program if a risk comes true or someone makes a mistake?

Agile and lean provide transparency for everything—the work, the status, who is doing what. If your organization is still blaming people for mistakes, you might have trouble being a servant leader.

My advice is to start by protecting the program.

"I am the Wall Around the Program"

We're sort-of agile. We have the idea of iterations, and we use kanban to see our work in progress. We're not perfect at getting to "done" all the time. And, our management still blames us if we don't make their *imposed* deadlines.

I decided the best way I could serve the software program was to protect the feature teams. I begged the program product owner to define reasonable interim deliverables. And, I would protect the feature teams from what I called "management mayhem."

My boss came over to me about halfway through the program and said, "I don't think your program is making enough progress. What are you going to do about it?"

I replied, "Nothing. I can't do anything about it. The teams are working to their maximum capacity. I need to change your mind and the other managers' minds about what we can accomplish in a month. Your expectations are not in line with reality."

He looked puzzled. I dragged him over to the product backlog burnup chart and the total feature burnup chart and explained that management had added more and more features without adding more time. "How realistic is this? I've been telling you for weeks now, you can add what you want, but the total time has to change. We are not magicians. You can see our progress is steady. Your additions are exponential. That's nuts."

He finally understood because of my charts. He agreed that management had unreasonable expectations.

I was the only one he spoke with, which made me happy. I get paid to deal with management, not to let the nonsense roll downhill. I was able to protect the program, which for me, was an act of servant leadership."

—*A software program manager where agile is still new*

11.5 Welcome Bad News

Part of listening is to welcome bad news, not just all news.

As program managers, we prefer to know that everything is going just fine. Few programs speed along with no bumps. When you make it easy for people to bring you bad news, you can hear and see the actual program status.

You cannot be everywhere and hear everything. You, as a program manager, have an obligation to see what's happening in your program, good and bad. Your problem is: how can you observe what teams do? Once you can see them, you might be able to generate several options for helping people bring you bad news.

11.5.1 *Visit every team, wherever they are*

I recommend you visit the feature teams. If you are all in one city or on one campus, consider Management By Walking Around and Listening (MBWAL) as in (BCD05). If people know you're wandering around every Tuesday and Thursday (as an example), they know they have an opportunity to discuss issues with you. You might even send an email, "I intend to wander around starting at 4pm on Thursday. Let me know if you would like me to drop by your team and discuss anything."

If the feature teams are all over the world, visit the teams who are remote from you at least once a quarter. Depending on the duration of your program, that might not be often enough. Yes, travel is time-consuming and can be expensive. It's more expensive to have insufficient communication and defects.

11.5.2 *Watch your facial expressions*

We all react to good and bad news. How you react can change the conversation.

"Think of Bad News as an Opportunity"

I had a program where two feature teams consistently missed their deliverables. MarComm was too busy with "other" things. I wanted to pull my hair out.

One day when I was tired, I grimaced and frowned at a program team meeting. The program product owner later asked me, "Do you want to hear bad news?" I said, "Of course!" "If you don't watch your facial expressions, you won't hear it," he said.

Uh oh. I reframed how I thought of bad news to an opportunity for improvement. I explained what I did at the next program team meeting:

"I would like to reframe our bad news into opportunities to improve. I welcome your 'bad news' and we will work together to capitalize on opportunities."

I decided I could look serious, but not upset. I started to say, "That's an opportunity for problem solving!"

It was corny, but it worked. I heard more bad news than I thought I could stomach, and we solved those problems fast.

—An experienced program manager

Sometimes, a change in your mindset can change your expressions. Sometimes, your expression can change your mindset. Make sure you are open to opportunities, even though sometimes those opportunities look like problems.

11.5.3 Consider an anonymous email box for suggestions

I don't normally like anonymous emails with suggestions. I would rather have a conversation. On the other hand, if people are having trouble and you don't hear about it, consider an anonymous email system. People can then email their concerns.

If you work in a low trust environment where you need an anonymous email box, you might have trouble with using agile for your program. You can develop more trust by being transparent about your work and delivering frequently. The more you deliver your work (fixing impediments, solving problems, acquiring resources such as labs, whatever your program needs), the more your program will trust you.

11.6 Use the Growth Mindset

Dweck describes the growth mindset in *Mindset: The New Psychology of Success*, (DWE07).

Fixed Mindset	Growth Mindset
You are born with fixed skills or talents.	Skills arise from hard work. You can improve.
Avoid challenges. In the face of challenge, give up easily.	Challenges are an opportunity. Persist until you get it right.
Coast by, don't bother with effort.	Effort is essential to mastery.
Get defensive with feedback.	Learn from feedback.
With setbacks, blame others. Get discouraged.	Setbacks are something you use to try harder the next time.
Feel threatened by others' success.	Find inspiration in others' success.

Figure 11.1: Comparison of Fixed and Growth Mindset

Agile and lean lend themselves to the growth mindset. Teams learn early by experimenting and discovering what works and what doesn't work.

If you decide you need to coach people on the program team or in the feature teams, consider using the growth mindset to help people see that they can succeed. They might need to learn how, and they can learn to do so.

11.7 Ask For the Results You Want

People live up or down to your expectations. If you expect the teams to ask you to solve each problem, they will. If you create a hierarchy where teams have to check with a quasi-manager (such as a Scrum Master or agile project manager), they will.

Instead, imagine what would happen if you say to the teams, "Please solve problems across the organization when you can, using your small-world networks and Communities of Practice."

People would talk to other people. They might email, IM, use whatever program/project wiki or electronic space you provide for collaboration. You can't know in advance what they will solve or not solve.

People and teams can still use their program manager, Scrum Master, or project manager to help solve problems. But, when you ask people to solve problems—and don't second-guess them—they will. Remember, you have adults working on your program. They pretty much know how to dress themselves, rent an apartment or buy a house, and raise children. They solve problems now. Expect them to do so at work.

When you ask people to solve problems, you can magnify momentum in your program.

Here are some guidelines I have found useful:

11.7.1 Set expectations for being stuck

Ask people to define how long they will work alone before they ask for help, in their teams or across the organization. My suggestion for this time is 30 minutes. That might seem short to you. I have found that if people spend a solid 30 minutes being stuck, as in they cannot think of an experiment to try or their search for an answer is fruitless, they stop working on this problem and read email or surf the web. They spend much more than 30 minutes being stuck.

If they don't ask someone to pair or ask the team to swarm on a problem once they've spent 30 minutes being stuck, the chances increase that they will spend a full day being stuck. They won't say anything until the standup—and even then, they might be reluctant to say anything in public.

Instead, if people have a guideline about being stuck, they may act before the day is gone.

You, as a program manager, can show others how to ask for help. Even if you don't need help, ask for it. When you set the example, people are more likely to ask for help.

11.8 Principles of Develop Your Servant Leadership:

1. Trust the people on the program team and the feature teams to do their jobs. The principle is: "Build projects around motivated individuals. Trust them to get the job done."
2. Look for and remove impediments that people cannot remove themselves. The principle is: "Empower the team."
3. Discover ways to encourage the teams to do better or more than you can imagine. The principle is: "The best architectures, requirements, and designs emerge from self-organizing teams."

CHAPTER 12

Shepherd the Agile Architecture

One of the big problems in agile and lean program management is how to manage the product's architecture. If you don't shepherd the architecture, you end up with a mess. If you create frameworks before you have features, you will be wrong. You might have significant rework (not refactoring) late in the program. Architecture throughout the program is the way we manage that risk. You might need to read Architects Can Help Expose Risks (page 148), and decide When Should You Consider Architectural Stories (page 153).

The risks of deciding on the frameworks up front are considerable in a program. On the other hand, no architectural guidance might be a disaster on your program. Consider how your program can create an iterative and incremental approach to architecture. Also consider when is the most responsible moment to decide on the product's architecture and the frameworks.

Back in How Often Can You Release Your Product? (page 71), you saw the potential for release frequency, based on the kind of product you have. Now, consider when to make architectural decisions.

The closer your product is to SaaS, the longer you can wait to make many architectural decisions. You might have to make product-guidance architectural decisions, but you often don't have to make many large up-front design decisions. The closer your product is to the right side of the continuum, with hardware, the more you might have to use set-based design approaches, or provide more architectural guidance earlier.

Software as a Service	Boxed Software	Product with Firmware	Software with Hardware or Mechanical components
Continuous			**Infrequently**
Continuous Deployment: As often as several times a day	Often: But the cost of release is still high	Less Often: The cost of release is high	Infrequently: Every release might be a major release

Architectural decisions and releasing costs less — Architectural decisions and releasing costs more

Last responsible moment is later — Last responsible moment is earlier

Figure 12.1: Release Frequency and the Cost of Architectural Decisions

The program architect should not decide alone. The program architect works with feature teams and other architects across the program to collaborate and decide when to select which frameworks.

That makes your program architect's job one of shepherding the business value of the architecture, which is a social and collaborative role requiring communications. The program architect helps facilitate the autonomy, collaboration, and exploration for the feature teams.

12.1 Architects Write Code

If we start with the premise that all architects on our program write code, we start well.

In software programs, we are accustomed to having enterprise, solution, or application architects. Often, those people do *not* sit with the project teams. Instead, they proclaim the architecture from afar, early in the program.

That doesn't work in agile or lean programs. It doesn't work in other programs either, but we can discuss that later, over a beverage of your choice.

In an agile or lean program, the architect is responsible for the business value of the architecture, not for telling people what to do. The program architect does this in many ways:

- Balances the short-term goals with the overall system integrity, risk, expediency, technical debt, anything else that you would trade off short term goals against.
- Sustains development against technical debt. For test systems, this is the age-old problem of testing versus automating the tests and how you automate the tests. I'm a huge fan of automate enough and refactor your way into what you need, because you may not know what you need until you see how the system under development evolves.
- Writes acceptance criteria for system qualities and quality scenarios for the product.
- Leads the definition of how a complex system is structured, organized, and implemented. Landing zones can help guide this effort.
- Works with a feature team in a hands-on way. No seagull architects. No PowerPoint architects, (See *Practices of an Agile Developer* for an excellent description of this, SH06). No prophets. No police. Agile architects develop code and develop tests.
- Works with users (or with the program product owner on behalf of the users) to understand what the users do, how the users work, what the users understand and don't understand about the system. What is the product vision? (See Develop the Program Vision, page 40, for more information.)

Architects work with the entire project team, not alone. Architects work on all parts of the product, not just the challenging or interesting parts. In fact, if there are rote parts or boring parts, maybe that's where the architect is needed most to automate something so humans don't have to do it.

In my workshops and in my executive briefings, I tell managers they should put their most talented people, aka architects, on the things that are agile or lean impediments. For complex programs, those are most often the build system and test automation. I suggest they use the architects for several iterations to make significant progress on those problems, and get to some version of done.

You may have different roles for your architect, especially if you are integrating Commercial Off the Shelf (COTS) software or vendor-supplied products:

- Act as editor-in-chief for architecture decisions on the team.
- Guide the individual feature team architects who do the actual work.
- Help establish new products that are based on the architecture. This means understanding re-use, and establishing a vision for how the architecture slowly evolves as new products come and go. Can we harvest frameworks and products from what we have now?
- Help the business people understand and take advantage of the architecture for new system features, third-party integrations, and new product lines. The architect might use the product vision to discuss the relative value of features with product owners and the value of frameworks with feature teams.

You can see that people who have architecture responsibility shepherd the *business value* of the architecture. This is not the traditional "I'll tell you how to build it because I know everything" position that way too many architects take.

12.2 Many Developers Become Architects

If architects write code, and if everyone owns the code, and we get to the final product by refactoring—which is how agile works—some substantial number of developers will work as architects at any given time. If your teams also pair or swarm over the code, no one will be able to tell who is the architect and who is not. That works quite well.

You still may need a program architect who can discuss risks with the business people, especially on the core team.

A program architect acts as a risk manager. She is experienced and able to talk with business and management with ease. She shepherds the business value of the architecture.

In Avoid Hierarchical Titles (page 84), I suggested you don't call a program architect a "chief" architect. You want the architect to identify with the program, not with the organization's hierarchy. When you use words such as *chief, master,* or *über,* you create or reinforce a hierarchy.

Architects may need to coach other developers, especially in how to create iterative and incremental designs—if they know how.

12.3 Encourage Iterative and Incremental Architecture

Many developers and architects see the big picture of the architecture, before they write any code. They know where they want to go and they want to implement the entire feature, *now.* That's not helpful in an agile and lean program.

Instead, request that the architects collaborate on evolving the picture of the architecture over time. If they see that they have "curlicue" features, request that the architects collaborate with the teams to simplify the teams and the features.

Sometimes, this might mean that the teams realize they don't have a cross-functional team that can deliver value. When the teams realize this, they will agitate for change. Program managers and program architects are technical leaders who can help the teams reorganize themselves, if necessary. See The Teams Have Dependencies on Other Teams (page 189) for an explanation of straight and curlicue features.

I have yet to see an architecture last from initial design through the end of a program unchanged. Maybe you have.

The risks of totally designing an architecture are too high for an agile and lean program. Help the architects learn how to create features iteratively and incrementally.

Here's one way to think about iterative and incremental architecture and design. Assume you have a product with a three-tier architecture. People have a picture of the architecture and while security pervades the product, the base security component is in the Platform layer.

As everyone creates features, it appears that the base security component is violating the Principle of Least Surprise and the Single Responsibility Principle. (The Principle of Least Surprise says that the product should act as the users expect it to. The Single Responsibility Principle says that one component should do one, and only one thing. Otherwise, you have coupling.)

This is a great time to refactor the code. Refactoring the code might not be sufficient when security violates two principles. And, you might refactor and discover performance problems. It's time for iterating on the architecture.

You have several options. Consider the options in Architects Can Help Expose Risks (page 148) and Break the Architecture with Purpose (page 154).

No one could tell at the beginning of the program that security—as you planned it—would be a problem. The more the teams create features and refactor to patterns, the less likely the product will have a brittle architecture. With features first, everyone can contribute to the architecture.

I recommend as part of the release criteria, the feature teams define any performance or reliability criteria for the product or a piece of the product.

12.4 Architects Can Help Expose Risks

Aside from iterative and incremental development, the program architect can help expose risks. Maybe it's worth the time for an architectural spike to learn about some area of the product? Back in Software is Learning, Not Construction (page 77), I said that we can learn about risks early to manage them.

Some product features are quite difficult to refactor in. These include scalability, some performance issues, and reliability to name just three. Don't proceed with just features when these quality attributes are critical to your product's success.

One way to manage these risks is to verify your roadmap has a walking skeleton (also known as the tracer bullet) approach to developing features. When you show feature teams and product owners the walking skeleton, they will ask, "How fast is this part?" or "How will this part scale from 300 to 30,000 users?" You now understand their system qualities for performance or scalability. You can adjust the system qualities as you proceed.

What if you need to know about some parts of the architecture first, because they will drive other program tradeoffs? You might. For example, in a smartphone, you might need to know the screen size because that will drive the common GUI decisions and the heat dissipation risks.

There are several options for this kind of a potential product problem. The solution you select might depend on the kind of product you have, based on your product's complexity. See Understand Your Product's Complexity (page 14). Here are some options that might work for you:

- Do a pre-program research project. Bring together enough people or teams to prototype the architecture that those people believe will support the product you need. Once you have enough information, start the program.
- Develop an architectural roadmap integrated with the program roadmap, so you create features and manage architectural risks as you proceed.
- Integrate architecture spikes with feature development. Maybe your program can still develop the operating system (the platform), and can answer other questions as you proceed.

The larger the program, the more you want to see architectural problems early. You can't do that if you can't show the product working. What would it take for your program to show a walking skeleton of working product? That is the question your product owners and architects can answer.

12.5 What the Program Architect Accomplishes Daily

Architects lead by doing. Sometimes they do the hard work to pay down technical debt that's been accumulating for years. Sometimes they do the hard work of seeing how the features are evolving into an eventual framework, or two or three. And, when you have 200 or 300 or 400 people on a program, all over the world, working in 2-week iterations, you may well need people who explore just ahead of feature teams, so that the feature teams are free to develop features.

There is a difference between agile on a small program of about three teams and agile on programs of more than 10 teams. Part of it is the communication paths. No matter how much you try to communicate, the larger program will have more communication issues, just because there are more people.

Coordinating the design and architecture among very large programs is a non-trivial task. It's partly managerial and partly technical. It's also social and communication work. See Architecture is a Social Activity (page 151).

Evolving the architecture is not a problem that a program can solve with hierarchy and maintain agility. And it is a difficult problem to solve. Communities of Practice can help.

Consider these options for an architect's daily work:

1. Use an architectural kanban based on the agile roadmap. Decide what risks the architecture wants to address now and how.
2. Perform architectural spikes with a feature team. This helps a team learn how the architect thinks about problems and solutions. In addition, working with a team spreads the architecture knowledge so everyone can work better.

3. Lead (and don't direct) an Architecture Community of Practice. What do you want people to know, to evolve the architecture in a coherent way? What architecture problems do you want to raise? What do other people want to raise and address?
4. Provide direct coaching to people who want it.
5. Work with people and teams across the organization so they understand how to use the current architecture and how to evolve it.

Your program architect might explore the boundaries of the current architecture and provide feedback to the program product owner. When it's time to change the boundaries, encourage the architect to work with a team, not alone. Everyone will benefit. See Martin Fowler's *Who Needs An Architect?*, FOW03 for a wonderful description of what architects might and should not do in an agile project.

12.6 Architecture is a Social Activity

Architecture is guidance that allows the feature teams to understand the general—and as the program proceeds—the more specific—patterns and frameworks to use. We hope that things don't change once we understand where we are headed.

However, because the feature teams make design decisions every day, we know that the architecture may have to adapt, if not change. The way the architects handle this change is with communications.

Instead of thinking of the architects as the people who define the architecture, encourage the architect to socialize her concerns about architecture. The architect can:

- Use Communities of Practice to help explore alternatives.
- Work with a feature team to spike a feature with architectural implications.
- Ask and encourage people across the program to discuss architectural qualities as they create features.

- Assess risks and architecture as the feature teams create features.
- Manage those risks to create a coherent product.
- Ask "how did the code change? How did the tests change?" when discussing refactoring and an incremental approach to architecture.
- Ask, "How will this scale from 300 to 300,000 users?," especially if the product owner wants a different scaling than anyone expected.

The program architect is a servant leader, coaching, influencing, and working across the program. The program architect learns from the teams and with the teams—the learning is not a one-way activity.

12.7 Problems You May Encounter With Architecture

What if your product owners want to fill your iterations with features and you don't have time to look ahead for architectural issues? Make your stories smaller.

You have several problems here. You have the Feature-itis (page 159) problem. Some teams may not have transitioned to agile well. Your architects may be PowerPoint architects. Feature-itis is an indication that a variety of people may not understand how to discuss business value. Does the program architect need to be part of the conversation about Rank Items in the Roadmap or Backlogs (page 60)? Sometimes, the architect can help the program product owner understand value better.

Consider these options:

1. If you are using iterations, make sure that the iterations are no longer than two weeks. If they are already two weeks, reduce them to one week. That will have the effect of reducing your story size. When you reduce your story size, people will shriek, and say, "We can't do that!" But you will discover either

the essence of the story, or the team will swarm around the story. Either is fine. If the architect can help reduce the batch size, everyone can see how to evolve the product towards the eventual frameworks.

2. Make sure every team provides an updated picture of the product architecture. Use the small-world networks to make sure every other team sees those pictures and agrees with them.

3. Ask the program architect to lead some architectural spikes to inform the product value team of the risks. These spikes will also inform the feature teams when it's time for them to work on those features.

4. Lead the effort to determine what an MVP is, and how to create a minimum walking skeleton.

Architects might have to work with the program manager to help create and use the small-world networks. Architects might have to work with the product owner value team to help create small-enough features or MVPs to show progress. Architects might work with feature teams to understand the risks of one alternative over another.

Can your architects work as servant leaders, focusing on the business value of the architecture rather than on what they think the architecture requires? This might be a fundamental role change for your architects.

When Should You Consider Architectural Stories?

Sometimes, the product owner needs to learn about tradeoffs for the product. Sometimes, the teams need *someone* to do an architectural spike to understand the risks and value of implementing one way or another.

Consider the following when composing architectural stories:

When you experiment, you have a specific learning goal in mind. You learn to manage the unknowns or risks. You might not want more feature development until you understand the tradeoffs of different architectures or frameworks.

This is different work than a story that starts, "As a developer" or "As an architect." When you have architectural stories or spikes, you have a specific learning goal that benefits someone, not just a developer or architect. The benefit is to the user. Do you want to learn about performance before you commit to a particular architecture or design? Your story might be something like this: "As an experienced user, I want to know that my search completes in under one second." You might have tests that test a variety of search types, results return, and how the lookup works given one size of data and another size of data. Then, the teams can explore because the product owner (maybe working with the architect) bounded the problem.

Architectural stories are not the problem. Stories that do not deliver value are the problem. Make sure everyone understands the value of the deliverable.

12.8 Break the Architecture with Purpose

Sometimes, the teams proceed through their work, evolving the feature design and the overall architecture. The teams encounter a decision point. To quote Yogi Berra, "When you come to a fork in the road, take it!"

People on the program might realize that to implement this feature, they need to break a current design pattern. They might realize that they have to trade off one architectural quality for another. Or, they might decide that they need some exploration to understand cost or duration for some feature or feature set.

It's time to explore some competing designs. Here are some options to consider:

1. Ask the program architect and at least one feature team to develop the questions the program needs answered. Are you trying to trade off architectural qualities (size, performance, or usability as three examples)?
2. Start an architecture experiment. What happens if we try it this way as opposed to the current way we are doing it?
3. Consider "competing" designs from different feature teams.

In each case, the program architect works with the team(s) to develop the answers the program needs. The program architect might lead the exploration as a servant leader.

When I say "competing" designs from different feature teams, the idea is to evaluate the pros and cons of the designs, not the team deliverables. Certainly, do not compare the teams.

Your program might decide to break the architecture. As long as they understand their goals, the questions they want to answer, and they timebox their work, this can create better architecture and design for your program. Ask the teams to manage the risks and report often on their progress.

12.9 Principles of Shepherd the Agile Architecture

1. Integrate architecture into what each team does, all the time. The principles are: "The best architectures, requirements, and designs emerge from self-organizing teams" and "Decide at the most responsible moment."
2. The larger the program and the more complex the product, the more you may have to consider some look-ahead exploration. The principles are: "Amplify learning" and "Build integrity in."
3. Expect the architecture to change. Ask the architects to learn from the feature teams as well as the feature teams learning from the architects. The principle is: "Continuous attention to technical excellence and good design enhances agility."

CHAPTER 13

Solve Program Problems

As a program manager, you will have plenty of program problems to solve. You will also need to help teams identify their problems. As a servant leader, you want to help people bring you bad news without feeling threatened or at risk. Let your teams know that you are there to help them with their obstacles, known or unknown, and not there to blame or punish them. Your teams will bring their problems to you earlier when you lead like this.

13.1 Ask For the Problems or Impediments First

When a team brings you a problem, ask these questions:

- What do you think is the cause of the problem?
- What have you tried already?
- Do you have impediments you need me/the program team/the core team to remove?

You don't have to ask these questions in this order. If your teams are anything like the people I've worked with in the past, they have an idea of what the problem is. They have tried some solutions. They need you to help in some way: Maybe they need some extra servers. Maybe you need a release/deployment team. Maybe it's something else.

A caution: Never say, "Don't bring me a problem without a solution." That's a management trap and prevents you from discovering and fixing problems early when they might be manageable. You might need to help the team(s) do root cause analysis, conduct a retrospective, or brainstorm multiple options if they are stuck. Your job as a servant leader is to help unstick the team. Make it easy for people to bring you their concerns.

Back in Continuous Integration and Testing Supports Collaboration (page 85), I explained my guidelines for trying to manage problems and remove impediments. Here are some guidelines for the program team problems and impediments:

1. Ask for the result you want.
2. Assume each person understands his/her problem better than you do. Ask that person to explain it to you, or to the program team.
3. Use the rule of three for each potential solution. See *Behind Closed Doors: Secrets of Great Management*, BCD05 for more information on how to use this rule for management problems.
4. Ask the program team for help in generating the solutions to these problems.
5. Never impose a solution. If no one is willing to volunteer to try a solution, assume it's not reasonable. Go back to the drawing board.

Some of the teams will need different initial solutions. Some teams will need help making their stories smaller. Some teams will need help learning to swarm around their features, so they finish features earlier in the iteration. That sets each team up for success for continuous integration.

But those impediments might be just the tip of the iceberg for your teams. Once you start generating some options, you can start to see what the costs are, and you can start comparing the value of those options.

Encourage teams to experiment with their potential solutions, especially if your program is in the Complex part of the Cynefin framework. You and the teams might not realize what the "perfect" solution is (if one even exists). Experimentation with measurement will help people realize what they might do to solve the problem. See Invite People to Experiment (page 88).

13.2 People on the Core Team Don't Deliver What They Promise

When people on the core team don't deliver, they put the entire program at risk. You can explain this when you ask them for commitments, as in Beware of Forgetting Core Team Members (page 27).

Maybe you have someone too senior, who can't commit to program-level work. Maybe you have someone too junior, who doesn't have the ability to do the work or the influence to complete it.

Use a one-on-one meeting, as in *Behind Closed Doors: Secrets of Great Management*, (BCD05), so you can learn what is happening for that person at work, and you can problem-solve together. Do not expect to solve a problem of people not delivering at a public meeting.

Use your servant leadership empathy and awareness to solve this problem. You might need to help someone learn how to deliver. You might need to ask for someone different for your program team. You might need to have a conversation with that person's manager or yours to solve the problem.

13.3 Your Product Owners Have Feature-itis

Feature-itis is when product owners decide they only want to know about features. The product owner does not want to rank technical debt, defects, anything that might interrupt the flow of features.

The problem is this: unless you have a brand new product, you are bound to have technical debt in any number of areas and already-existing defects that have been around for years.

You can choose to ignore that work. You can tell the teams to ignore that work. When the teams address technical debt and defects, they fix things to make it easier for the team to work faster in the future. If your product owners want to ignore fixes, they will slow the team's momentum. If several product owners do this, your program can screech to a halt.

What can you do instead?

Make sure the stories that the product owners write with the teams are small. Sometimes, product owners want to ignore fixing work because they think the teams gold-plate the features. The smaller the story, the less likely anyone will gold-plate.

If your teams deliver stories into the product every day or so, the product owner can see if the team is gold-plating. When the product owner trusts the team, the product owner can relax about the issue of ranking technical debt and defects.

As for the teams, unless you have a reason to create technical debt, tell them you don't want them to. If you have a short-term deadline, maybe you can have some debt. But, then decide when the team can pay the debt down.

Teams should not be creating defects as they finish features. They need to get the feature to done. If teams can't do that, they need to understand what their problems are, and address them.

Product owners need to review the backlog of technical debt and defects, in addition to features on the roadmap. Teams need a way to keep their code and tests healthy.

Discuss the business value of every item in the backlog, not just features.

13.4 People on Teams Are Multitasking

If you have people multitasking on your program and another project, your program will be delayed. You will incur a Cost of Delay that will affect when you can release the entire product.

Teams need to learn how to manage support work in their kanban or in their iterations. If product owners want a team to "do more," the only way to do that is to make the stories smaller. With smaller stories, it's possible to finish and maintain a sustainable pace, a rhythm to your work.

If teams have a ton of support work for a previously released product that is not part of *this* program, that is a risk to your program. You may have to address that with the people who want the support.

Do you have people pulled off onto other projects? That is a sign of a management team who is not managing the project portfolio. If you are tracking run rate, this is a huge problem. Your program is paying (silently) for other project or program work.

I have done these things in the past:

1. Measured the Cost of Delay so my managers understood why multitasking was a problem.
2. Asked the teams to shorten their iterations, so they could only commit to a smaller number of stories. I asked them to track new stories that they had not committed to. I brought that data with me to the Operations Committee review meeting and explained why the program was late. This provided the transparency we needed.
3. Asked team members to come to me if anyone wanted them to do something not on the program. I would then take the request and assess it.

You may have other options. Your first job is to make the multitasking transparent.

Multitasking will slow your program and stop people from making progress. Don't allow it.

13.5 How to Start a Program With More People Than You Need

You're starting a program. Your organization recognizes you have a program. Your management team makes sure you have all the people you need *right now*. And, your program is not ready for them. Your eventual 150- or 200-person program does not need more than a couple of 5-to-7-person teams right now, maybe even fewer. What do you do?

Ask the people to self-organize into collocated cross-functional teams. If you are working on extensions to an already-existing product, ask them to select a backlog of defects from the defect-tracking system. Their job in the next two weeks is to: 1, fix the defects; and 2, determine what they do not have as a process or tools for proceeding for the program. If you are working on a brand new product, ask them to work on an already-existing product with the same tools they will be using for the new product. If they will be working on a brand new product with brand new languages and tools, ask them to create the equivalent of "Hello World" with the new languages and tools.

Maybe they discover they have technical debt in unit or system tests. That means that technical debt goes on the program backlog, at the very top. Maybe they discover they don't have sufficient access to the build system or the version control system. Good to know now, before they start on features. Or, they will discover they need training or new machines or licenses for the new tools. Good to know before they start in earnest.

Maybe they cannot create collocated cross-functional teams. They get to decide how to organize themselves, or tell you or a project manager that they have a problem they need help solving.

The idea is that at the end of the first two-week iteration, you know where the initial set of team-based risks are. Every project and program has them. The larger the program, the more those risks hide so Murphy can spring them on you just when you don't need them. When you have everyone, let all those people discover the risks for you. Now you have fodder for your risk list and the teams know their impediments. Everyone wins.

"Consider a Hackathon"

I have had "excess" team members do a hackathon to start building automated test approaches and harnesses, prototype new ways of getting to the desired functionality, maybe start the Continuous Delivery pipeline. There are many things these folks can do to benefit the program.

—*Paul Ellarby, program manager*

You could also do a Hudson Bay Start, as in *Manage It! Your Guide to Modern, Pragmatic Project Management*, (ROT07) on the program itself. But you almost certainly do *not* need all 200 people for that.

Whatever you do, do not let all those people hamper the program's progress by starting on the program—unless you really can use them all.

As part of this first iteration, ask the program product owner to build an agile roadmap and backlog. In my experience, too few program product owners are ready with an agile roadmap at the start of the program. But to not have any idea where you're going? Not good.

If you start in with Iteration Zero, you can spend your life in Iteration Zero, Iteration Minus One, and so on. That's death for your program. I like to spend a day or so starting. But not much more. Even for large programs. People need to recognize the urgency of starting and delivering.

Once the program product owner has the agile roadmap, all the product owners can work with this product owner to generate the first ranked backlog for all the teams. Now, at the end of the first iteration, the program has these deliverables:

- Everyone knows where they have technical debt in unit or system tests.

- Everyone knows if they have adequate tooling for working on the product.
- If they are geographically distributed, they know if they can communicate with each other.
- The program product owner has an agile roadmap.
- The product owners have ranked backlogs for their teams.
- The teams have practiced working together, releasing something.
- The core team has completed the program charter, so the teams now know what the program vision and release criteria are.

Not shabby for two weeks, is it?

13.6 Principles of Solve Program Problems

1. Make sure you know what's going on with the people on your program team. Use one-on-ones to solve problems privately. The principle is: "Face-to-face conversation is the most efficient and effective method of conveying information."
2. Do not start a program with more people than you can plan for at the beginning. Find a way for those people to contribute while you get ready. The principle is: "Build integrity in."
3. Make sure your program team can meet in person to learn how to work together. The principle is: "Face-to-face conversation is the most efficient and effective method of conveying information."

CHAPTER 14

Integrating Hardware Into Your Program

When your product has more than software—it has mechanical or hardware components—you might not see how to use agile and lean approaches to see the product evolve and get feedback on it. You might not be able to use agile and lean externally, for customers. You might only be able to use agile and lean internally, to help create the best product possible. You can use the principles of agile and lean to see product and provide feedback, using incremental design, integrating early, and seeing demonstrations of the entire product as early and often as possible.

The only thing that's inherently sequential with non-software parts of a product is when they are ready for physical form. Every time the engineers create a physical form for a part, it costs money. That money is called non-recurring engineering (NRE) expenses.

NREs are part of your program's costs. You, as a program manager, might have to manage those costs as well as any other costs you have. It's possible those costs are a risk for your program.

14.1 Hardware Risks Are Different Than Software Risks

Hardware and software product development both face common risks:

- We might not know how to solve the problem. We need more research before development.

- We might have to iterate to understand how best to solve the problem(s).
- We need to obtain feedback often enough to know if we are solving the problems in a way that works.

The risks associated with hardware are different than than those associated with software. The "problem" with hardware is that the hardware cycles are not homogeneous. That is, the risks of mechanical work are on a different cycle than the risks of analog or digital work. The different kinds of hardware iterate with simulators at different times. They go to physical form at different times.

One big question for your program is this: Will you gain any benefit from early-and-often physical form for learning? The program will incur more cost. Is it worth the value?

14.2 Understand Cost and Value for Hardware

Back in Software is Learning, Not Construction (page 77), I discussed the idea that software is learning, never construction. Much of hardware development is also learning.

In addition to the learning, part of hardware development is being ready for manufacture, for fabrication of the final design. In highly complex hardware programs, design for manufacturing might be its own small program.

Because we learn so much when we marry the software with the hardware, one question to ask is this: When is the right time to start developing physical prototypes? The prototype will have some cost. What is the value the program could receive from that learning?

Often, the hardware and software teams use design by contract to determine what to do where—the interface between the hardware and software. The earlier the hardware people deliver prototypes, the faster the teams can learn if the design is correct. The teams shorten the feedback loops. Is that learning worth the cost of the prototype?

One way to think about this value is to consider the Cost of Delay. How much longer will it take to finish the product if the software teams can't start until hardware is done? What if hardware has to revise their designs based on feedback from software? Consider the questions in Integrate Hardware Often (page 173).

Here's an example of how to consider costs. Imagine you have one hardware team and three software teams, a relatively small program. What is the cost for you to wait until the ninth month of a twelve-month program for a prototype?

Maybe your prototypes cost $10,000 each. Assume you get two prototypes, one for the hardware team and one to share with the software teams, a total of $20,000. Let's assume you find at least two problems in the first week that create a one-week delay in your program. Assume people cost $75/loaded labor hour. You have 16 people in the software teams and five people in the hardware team. That's a total of 21 x $75 x 40 for a one-week delay: $63,000.

Compare that cost to iterating earlier on the hardware.

I have no idea if you can create a prototype for $10,000. Your NREs might be much higher. It's possible that a chip could cost upwards of $1,000,000 and take at minimum, six weeks. In that case, see some alternatives in Manage Hardware Risks (page 174).

If you have a program of about 12 months, do you need to see a physical prototype before the last three months, a traditional time to prototype and then pilot? It depends on your risks.

You will incur some form of cost (NRE) whenever you have hardware go to physical form. The question is this: What is the value of that physical form to the overall program? What are the risks of iterating in physical form?

Remember, if you go to physical form earlier, you might be able to end the program earlier. That's because the product is sufficient as is. That doesn't happen often, but it does happen.

14.3 **Understand Each Part's Value**

Let's assume you are developing a robot. The machine has mechanical arms, a custom board with the robot's operating system on it, and one FPGA (Field-Programmable Gate Array) to customize the robot's use for you.

You will have these engineering components for your robot program:

- Mechanical work to create the arms
- Silicon board
- Operating system
- FPGA

The software teams can create the operating system in an agile way, because the operating system is all software. However, the operating system has interactions with the board, the FPGA, and how the arms work. The software teams can't wait until the mechanical and engineering teams complete their work. The software teams need to start work now.

None of the components have much value by themselves. However, they have tremendous value when they all work together.

The product roadmap will specify the relative value of each component. The teams need the roadmap to determine when to have each component and feature set of each component ready for the other teams.

This is tricky. The teams need to deliver the most important and valuable components first. Here is what a first quarter roadmap might look like. (My robot experience is quite old, so this is a fabricated roadmap.)

Because the mechanical, electrical, FPGA, and software can't integrate from the beginning, this roadmap looks a little like a kanban with swim lanes. You might not like *this* roadmap. You might like to organize your roadmap in some other way. Here are the principles I used:

Possible One Quarter Agile Roadmap for a Robot

Internal Release 1: Component Demo only		Internal Release 2: Component Demo Only		Internal Release 3: Joint Demos	
Mechanical: Joint exploration/R&D	Mechanical: Joint exploration/R&D	Joint Design, features 1-4 in emulator	Joint Design, features 5-6 in emulator	Create physical prototype in lab	Simulate OS input to current joint design
Silicon: First phase layout to check for heat and performance	Silicon: First phase layout to check for heat and performance	Silicon: Simulate Driver input, features 1-3	Silicon: Simulate Driver input, features 4-8	Silicon: Simulate Driver input, features 9-12	Silicon: Verify current features against all other work to date
OS: Interrupt and driver interactions, features 1-3	OS: Interrupt and driver interactions, features 1-3	Interrupt handler, features 1-5	Interrupt handler, features 6-10	Diagnostics basic features, 1-3	Diagnostic and Alarm integration
FPGA: Boot functions, 1-3	FPGA: Stop functions, 1-2	FPGA: Stop functions, 3-5	FPGA: Alarm, features 1-4	FPGA: Alarm, features 5-8	Integrate Alarm with Diagnostics
Program Concerns: Develop landing zones	Program Concerns: Iterate on landing zones	Program Concerns: Design review (OS, FPGA) to date	Program Concerns: Design review (Silicon & FPGA)	Program Concerns: Functional review to date (All)	Joint demo: FPGA & OS

Figure 14.1: One Quarter Agile Roadmap for a Robot

- Make the interdependencies transparent.
- Demonstrate the product as early as possible, even if it's via a breadboard.

Notice that some of the basic hardware and mechanical work takes just one two-week iteration. If the product owner realizes that the work will take longer—maybe the people who make the parts the team expected to use no longer produce those parts—he or she would change the roadmap to show that delay.

The roadmap makes the value visible. There will be feature sets you don't need at the start of the program. If the product owner and the teams work by value, it will be easier to see when it's time to invest in physical form and when you can wait.

14.4 See the Work

Sometimes, the mechanical and electrical engineering teams can feel like a black hole to the rest of the organization. I've heard statements such as, "We're working on the keyboard. We'll have it for you in a couple of months." They might. My experience is what we get in a couple of months is the first prototype of several we need. That's not finished work.

One way to see the work is to ask the engineers to use a kanban board. I recommend each component have its own kanban to see the work in progress.

A mechanical engineering kanban might look like this picture.

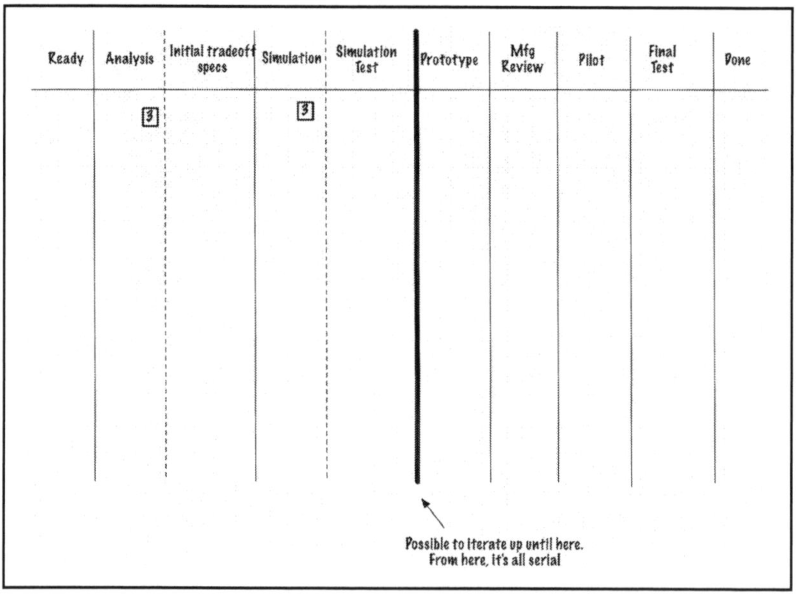

Figure 14.2: Possible Mechanical Engineering Kanban

A silicon engineering kanban might look like this picture.

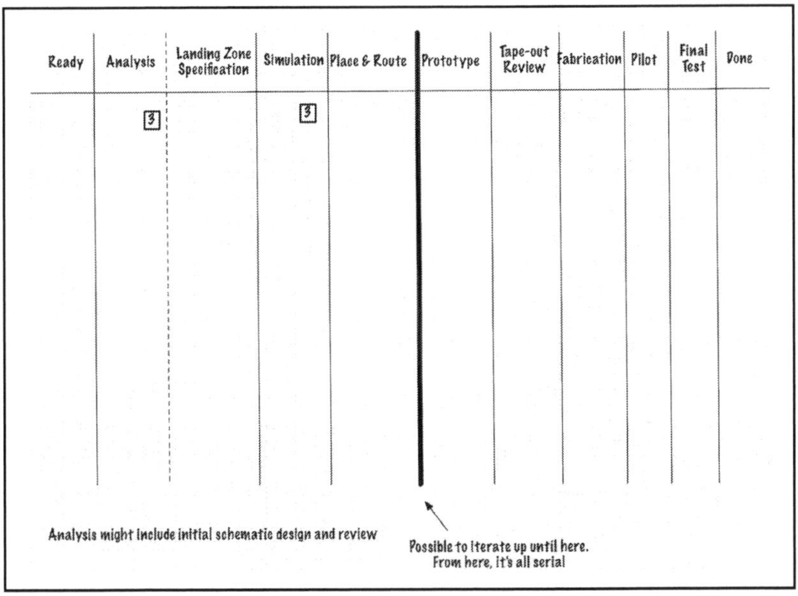

Ready	Analysis	Landing Zone Specification	Simulation	Place & Route	Prototype	Tape-out Review	Fabrication	Pilot	Final Test	Done
	3		3							

Analysis might include initial schematic design and review

Possible to iterate up until here. From here, it's all serial

Figure 14.3: Possible Silicon Kanban

An FPGA kanban might look like this picture.

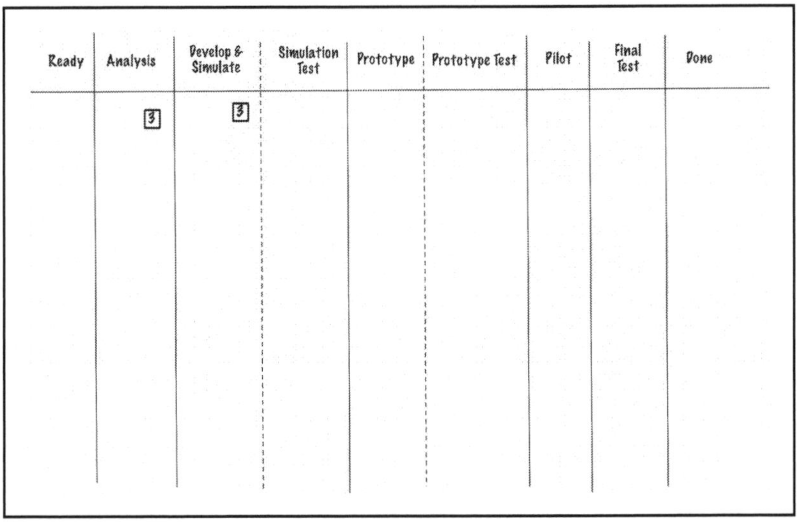

Ready	Analysis	Develop & Simulate	Simulation Test	Prototype	Prototype Test	Pilot	Final Test	Done
	3	3						

Figure 14.4: Possible FPGA Kanban

The FPGA kanban might look much more like a regular software kanban, up until you make the decision to go to physical form.

14.5 Design Incrementally and Iteratively

Mechanical engineers and hardware engineers iterate on their designs. It's easy and inexpensive to iterate with simulators and emulators.

Mechanical engineers use simulators to build and check their work. So do analog and digital engineers. They can use a simulator to walk step-by-step through their part of the product.

If you ask the mechanical and electrical engineers to design iteratively and incrementally—before they commit to physical form— you can then ask for continuous design review.

14.6 Use Continuous Design Review

Mechanical and hardware engineers can use continuous integration for their work as they simulate. They can apply those principles of seeing feedback continuously with the rest of the program when they use continuous design review.

In Encourage Iterative and Incremental Architecture (page 147), I suggested the teams evolve the *picture* of the architecture before finalizing their architectural decisions. Your software team might choose to have a design review of the architecture after three features. (See *Manage It! Your Guide to Modern, Pragmatic Project Management*, ROT07 for a fuller discussion of implementing several features before selecting an architecture.)

You can do that for the hardware pieces of your product. Depending on how long the engineers expect the hardware effort(s) to take, you might ask them to review the designs every week or every other week, if they work in two-week timeboxes.

As the engineers modify their original designs and determine what they can do in the mechanical or hardware parts of the product, they can explain their decisions to the software feature teams and/or architects.

14.7 **Integrate Hardware Often**

The cost of moving to physical form is high with mechanical and silicon components. However, if the program waits until the very end to marry all the components into a product, you will encounter the 90% Done schedule game. (That's where you have finished 90% of the work and have the other 90% remaining.) (See *Manage It! Your Guide to Modern, Pragmatic Project Management*, ROT07 for more information on this schedule game.)

The more integration points your program has, the easier it is to see the entire product, not just one component.

Hardware and mechanical engineering are on different cycles from each other, and they are each different from software. Even with each discipline, the risks are different when the teams collaborate together on one deliverable and when the entire program has to collaborate to create a product.

The engineering teams simulate to see problems in their own work and solve those problems. Each team is ready for integration at a different time. They can't integrate until they go to fabrication. That changes the feedback cycle(s) for the entire program.

Questions you can ask:

- Is there an interim physical form that would provide us value?
- How much does that form cost us to create?
- How long is it that prototype good for?
- If there is not an interim physical form that would provide us value, how can we obtain value and reduce risks with what kind of form or demonstration?

Here are some sample problems you could test for and avoid with early prototypes:

- The footprint is too large/too small.
- The design by contract work you thought was good turns out to be wrong.
- You have a design that works but doesn't produce the product you want.

Those are examples. You may have other problems.

14.8 Manage Hardware Risks

Because the hardware parts run on different cycles than the software parts, we have at least two ways to manage these risks: set-based design (See *What is Set-Based Design?* SIN09) and landing zones (*See Starting with Landing Zones*, (WIR11).

In set-based design, the designers iterate on the design. As they proceed, they rule in or out designs that do not intersect with the rest of the design components. In landing zones, the designers discuss the parameters of what makes a successful design and then converge on that success.

Both of these appear to be more like "implement several features and see what architecture emerges, rather than design up front." It's also about using the intelligence of an entire team.

There's a third option: is there a cost-effective way to make a prototype that can provide you with feedback without having all the properties? For example, can you use a 3D printer to check the physical footprint, even if you can't check heat dissipation? I don't know if that would work for your program or would be a waste of time. I do know that 3D printing is much faster than going to fab for many parts of your product.

I used a fourth option some years ago. We wanted to simulate the traffic on an internal network to see if the design we had would work. I asked about 20 people to meet the architect and me (I was the program manager) in a large conference room. We organized the people according to the types of traffic.

We had a metronome to help people walk on time. We simulated the network traffic—what was going where and when—with people. It wasn't a perfect test, and it told the architect a ton of information about how the software would work with the current hardware. I'm not sure we would do that now—we did not have adequate simulators back then. At the time, it was a cheap and useful approach to help the architect realize that the hardware would not integrate with the software as he desired.

These methods are not infallible. However, they all provide feedback faster and better than waiting until the end of the project/program, when you have spent all the money and time—and you still don't have hardware that works.

14.9 Develop the Software Before the Hardware Is Available

I have seen many programs develop the hardware at the same time as the software, or even in advance. The software and hardware people agree on designs in advance, and write them down. This is a form of "design by contract."

However, there is another alternative—to develop the software before the hardware. One of my reviewers, Ian Brockbank, said it this way:

> For the last twelve years I have worked for a company which develops audio chips, which have acquired more and more functionality over the years. We had an implicit assumption that the silicon was the most important part of the development, with software almost as an afterthought. After several projects where the software wasn't ready until a year or more after the silicon (and one program which ended up being cancelled after two chips and 4 years of development because no-one could use it without a major extra investment in software which the company wasn't able to make) we finally recognized that in some cases there is much more work on the software side than the hardware side. We are now getting to the point of starting software development long before there is hardware available.
>
> One of the most important things to do to allow this is to have abstractions which can act sufficiently well

to test the software in advance of the hardware. We use a range of abstractions with different levels of fidelity, from a simple array, through emulation libraries and simulators to FPGA instantiations of early versions of the chip, and we have found you can do a lot with a very low-fidelity abstraction. We have developed an advanced chip configuration package in the main using little more than an array behind a mocking layer for the communications. We develop advanced signal processing algorithms for embedded DSP cores with bit-exact emulation libraries on the PC. Only once it works in emulation do we consider trying it against real hardware.

Of course, this provides a provisional version of the software, which is only as good as the understanding of how the hardware works, so we always need to verify once the real hardware is available. Testing against FPGAs comes next. These allow us to test early versions/subsets of the chips against the software, and allow the interfaces to be validated, debugged, and refined before committing to the expense of a full mask set and fabrication run. It does take work to allow silicon designs to be suitable for FPGA—the porting is a full-time role even with suitable silicon designs---but it definitely pays for itself if it saves even a single respin, which can cost millions of dollars and (even worse) put the programme back by months.

Once the real silicon returns, there is still further verification work—the timing on FPGA is never exactly the same as the silicon, and there is analogue performance to consider as well, but in my experience even the simplest abstractions can cut out 80-90% of the dependence on real hardware during development and save months or even years on the project timeline."

—*Ian Brockbank, private communication*

Can you develop the software before the hardware? Is it a possibility for your program? What would have to be true for you to do so?

14.10 Principles of Integrating Hardware Into Your Program

1. Decide when it makes sense to move to physical form. Early and often, or later? The principle is: "See the whole."
2. Encourage working product. The principle is: "Deliver early and often to satisfy the customer."
3. Encourage technical discussion of architecture and design. The principle is: "Continuous attention to technical excellence and good design enhances agility."

CHAPTER 15

Troubleshooting Agile Team Issues

As a program manager, you will see many kinds of problems in the teams. Some of them are process problems—how can the team be better at agile or lean to deliver value better or faster? Sometimes, the people on the teams don't know how to be a team or how to diagnose their team problems.

You may see these problems or you may have to ask the team to self-assess to see the problems. You can troubleshoot these problems.

Remember, you are a servant leader. Grease the skids, eliminate the impediments, empower people to solve problems themselves.

15.1 The Teams Are Not Feature Teams

I've seen component teams and single-function teams attempt to work in an agile way. That might be better than what they did before, but it's not agile.

Unless you release libraries, component teams do not ship running, tested features. They need to organize along with several other component teams to release running, tested features. If your product is libraries, you need component teams.

Single-function teams violate the agile tenet that the team is cross-functional and has all the roles it needs to finish features.

Component teams and single-function teams create interdependencies.

If you have a ton of interdependency issues between teams, you might have the problem that teams are organized around architecture and not around features.

Most of the component and single-function teams I have seen are a legacy from the organization's waterfall days. How the heck are you going to create features, and integrate a feature every day, working across the architecture instead of through it? That is a huge impediment. If you have component teams, it's even more important that they work on small stories. That's because the teams will have a difficult time getting the stories done through the architecture.

Don't ask people to reorganize first. Instead, ask people to experiment. I have had good results asking people to experiment to see what works with self-organization, to pair or to swarm. When you ask, explain why you recommend these alternatives: multiple eyes on the code, everyone works together to reduce WIP and move a feature across the board, and whatever results you want.

15.1.1 *Ask the teams to experiment with self-organization around features*

- Explain to the teams that this is an experiment that "we as an organization are running for the next x weeks." Make x be short, as in one or two weeks.
- The only measure of success is running tested features. Managers do not compare teams. If managers compare teams, the experiment will not work. This is an experiment that the organization is going to learn from. Some teams will have small and easy features. Some teams will not. This is not a competition. If anyone compares teams, the teams will game this measure and you will lose the learning.
- Stop multitasking. Get everyone to work on just one project at one time right now. I know, this might be the most difficult

thing your organization has tried. Ignore the fact you need experts everywhere. Assign people to only one project.

- Ask the component teams to self-organize as feature teams for now. No changing managers. No changing desks. They get to decide how. If you are a manager, no decreeing who is a feature team with whom. If you have single-function teams, ask them to self-organize as feature teams for now.
- Ask the product owners to make the stories as small as they can make them, preferably one or two team-days in size or less. Tell the teams that if they don't have the expert they need for a story, that's okay. They can pair, swarm, or mob together to get the story done. But, they are not allowed to interrupt another team.
- Create an agile roadmap of the features you want in which internal release.
- The teams work on their backlog, or work in flow for this week or two weeks (not any longer) to see what happens when everyone works in feature teams of their own making and no one multitasks, to get features to done. Remember, this is an experiment.
- Have the teams do retrospectives themselves at the end of the short timebox so you can see what happens. Managers might need to supply retrospective facilitators.
- Decide what to do next. This is an experiment.

At the end of the experiment, ask the teams to assess the experiment, using these questions:

1. What happened?
2. Were the experimental feature teams able to release features?
3. What happened to the teams who needed experts?
4. What was challenging about this experiment?
5. What succeeded with this experiment?
6. What failed with this experiment?

7. What did you learn from this experiment?
8. What will you do in the future?

This is one way to help teams learn how to collaborate and explore with each other.

15.1.2 Ask the teams to pair around features

When you pair, two people work together to finish a piece of work. Traditionally, two developers paired. The "driver" writes the piece of work. The other person, the "navigator," observes the work and provides review, as the two people complete the work. As they work together, they trade places, say every 15-20 minutes.

Arlo Belshee wrote a great article called *Promiscuous Pairing and Beginner's Mind: Embrace Inexperience*, (BEL06) where he explains how you don't need to be an expert to be an effective pair or pair member.

When team members pair for features, they deliver. They focus. If they need help, they don't get stuck, because there are always two people working on one feature, discussing what to do next.

Encourage different varieties of pairing: developer/developer; developer/tester; or even a triad, which starts to look like a swarm.

15.1.3 Ask the teams to swarm around features

When teams swarm, the entire team works towards finishing a feature. Sometimes, teams split into smaller chunks, where people work on what they can, and then rejoin the team. Sometimes, they all work together, as in mob programming.[1]

When I teach one of my agile workshops, I challenge people to take one feature as a team and complete it within one hour.

Some teams do it by having the product owner explain what the feature is in detail. Then the developers pair and the tester(s) write

---

[1] http://www.mobprogramming.org

tests, both automated and manual. They all come together at about the 45-minute mark. They see if what they have done works. (It often doesn't.) Then the team starts to work together, to really swarm. "What if we do this here? How about if this goes there?"

Some teams work together from the beginning. "What is the first thing we can do to add value?" (That is an excellent question.) They might move into smaller pairs, if necessary. Maybe. Maybe they need touchpoints every 15-20 minutes to re-orient themselves to say, "Where are we?" They find that if they ask for feedback from the product owner, that works well.

If you first ask, "What is the first thing we can do to add value and complete this story?" you are on the right track.

Note how with pairing and swarming, people don't get stuck. They reduce their WIP. They deliver.

15.2 Teams Think They Are Agile, But They Are Not

There are many examples of teams thinking they are agile. Some have hardening sprints. Some organizations have development teams and testing teams. What I see often is developers working on one feature, followed by testers working on that same feature. A hardening sprint is an example of testers and developers working to finish the software, to get it to done.

Help the teams learn how to get each story to done in one or two days.

15.2.1 The team works in sequential iterations of developer/tester

Teams work in sequential iterations, where first there is one iteration of development for two weeks, and then one iteration of testing for two weeks. If you are like some of my clients, you even overlap the first week of testing, but you have one week of testing that extends

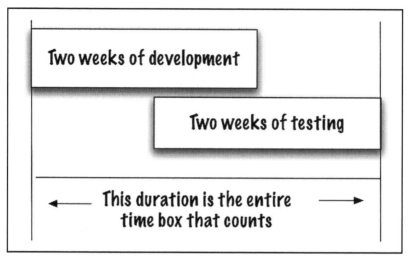

Figure 15.1: Staggered Development and Testing

beyond the last week of development. I didn't show that in this picture. That would extend the total timebox by another week.

When we look at the picture of Staggered Development and Testing, it doesn't matter how long the development or the testing iterations are. It matters how long the sum of the iterations are. If each iteration is two weeks, then the sum is four weeks. If you spend two weeks developing and three weeks testing, you have a five week iteration. It takes five weeks to get feedback and to know if the feature you developed is good. The feature isn't done until the testing is done.

You can Ask the teams to experiment with a self-organization around features (page 180). You might ask the teams to swarm around features. You might ask the teams to pair around features (page 182). Those are just three options.

Maybe something else would work for your environment.

Remember, if the testing occurs after the development, the developers are already onto the next features. The team incurs a delay in the feedback. The developers incur a delay because of the multitasking: stopping what they work on now, fixing the problem, and returning to the feature under development. Avoid staggered development and testing. Teams that stagger their development and testing find continuous integration or providing a continuous flow of value difficult, if not impossible.

In the program team, ask the product owners to reduce the feature size. The smaller the feature, the more the team can collaborate together to keep the feedback loop small and succeed at delivering.

15.2.2 *Some teams have hardening sprints*

Hardening sprints are a tremendous risk to your program.

Hardening sprints are an indication of incomplete work. Teams did not get their features to "done" in the committed time. People can make mistakes in their estimation. But, if teams need hardening sprints, they need to change their approach. They have technical debt and that debt may become a program-level risk.

If you have teams who discover and fix feature defects late in the game—when the team thinks that feature is complete—you have added a tremendous risk to your program. The developers multitask—they stop work on the feature they are working on now, return to a previous feature where they might not remember all the context, fix it—and then return to the feature they were working on.

As a program manager, watch for these problems. You will see it in feature teams not completing features they expected to, or in feature teams saying they need time to fix defects or perform hardening sprints.

Suggest that the team measure their cumulative flow to show where the work is.

Make it easy for people to bring you bad news. Do not be nasty about this problem. Help people be honest about where they are in their agile or lean journey.

Hardening sprints or fixing defects in a feature long after it was created are two examples of a similar problem: not getting to done on stories. There can be many reasons for this: insufficient testing, insufficient test automation, partial teams, people multitasking—to name just a few.

As a program manager, encourage the feature teams to perform retrospectives and discover why they have these problems. In addition, encourage the product owners for those feature teams to make the stories smaller. Smaller stories will help the teams see their problems faster and fix them faster. A hardening sprint does not allow you to have releasable product at all times.

Know if you have partial teams or people multitasking on your program, especially if you have target dates or a target budget. Your risks rise with partial teams or multitasking.

15.2.3 *You have partial feature teams*

A feature team has all the roles it needs to create features. It's a cross-functional team, of no more than nine people. (I prefer teams of 4-6 people.)

You might not have feature teams because a team might be missing testers, user experience people or database admins. The team is missing some role or roles and cannot complete features by itself.

You might have this problem because the organization was "lopsided" to start. The managers, before you started to use agile, thought it was fine to have many developers and "share" testers, user experience people, or DBAs. In a serial life cycle, maybe it was okay. It's not okay in agile.

Don't add teams of developers and create incomplete lopsided teams.

You don't get more throughput with extra developers without additional testers or business analysts or writers or whatever makes a cross-functional team in your organization. If your developers can work alone and produce features *by themselves*, okay. I have yet to see developers do that, and not be blind to their own defects.

What you care about in your program is the throughput of running tested features. You don't want partial teams to create work in progress. That's waste.

Partial feature teams is an artifact of waterfall thinking, optimizing for resource efficiency as in *This is Lean: Resolving the Efficiency*

Paradox, MOA13. Your management wants to throw people at the product. Don't let them.

If everyone is agile, you may not need as many people as your management thinks you do. You have continuous integration. You have feature teams. Don't start with more people than you need. Say, "Thank you. The program doesn't need more people than we can have on fully staffed feature teams. Unless you can staff feature teams with testers and product owners, I can't use these developers. They will slow us down. Thank you, anyway."

Emphasize that you want flow efficiency, moving features—deliverables—through the program.

If that doesn't convince them, estimate the Cost of Delay for partial teams, as in *Diving for Hidden Treasures: Finding the Value in Your Project Portfolio* (RE14). This is when you say, "At some point, we will need testers for those developers," or whatever role you are missing. "At that time, either we have a delay while we try to integrate someone into the team, or we will have to ask people to multitask. That delay, which I estimate to be some-number, will affect the entire program."

15.2.4 *You need experts to complete a story*

If you are in the midst of your transition to agile, you have plenty of experts. You may not have people who are generalizing specialists—people who specialize in one area and are capable of flexing their intellectual muscles in related areas.

Here's an example of what I mean by a generalizing specialist. As a developer, I loved writing platform and middleware layers. I was not so excited about the user interface. I specialized in the platform and secondarily in the middleware.

However, a feature isn't a feature unless the user can see it. I needed UI skills. I worked hard, and often with other people, to develop a sufficient knowledge of what constituted reasonable UI approaches. I often worked with UI designers who used paper prototypes to determine what the UI would be. I had guidelines. I was able to create features.

I went from a specialist in the platform to being a "full-stack" developer. I would never call myself a UI guru. On the other hand, with some help across the organization, I could create features.

There are other kinds of specialists, such as Database Admins, or people who just do the financials, or diagnostics. These people have focused on one area of the code base. They might be able to create features, but only in that area.

Teams without specific knowledge in one area are often reluctant to change code in that area. Or, the team may want to wait for an expert. You have another risk, another Cost of Delay.

Teams have to learn to become the experts they need to be to be able to help build features across the code base. They may find this quite difficult.

You can help in several ways:

- Acknowledge that this work will be difficult for the team.
- If the expert is available, ask the expert to work with the team in a short timebox, such as one week, to transition the expert's knowledge to the team. Make sure the expert works with the team for that timebox, and then the expert transitions away. If the team needs further help, can the expert have office hours for the team to call him or her? The goal is to not need the expert any longer.
- Ask the team members to pair around features they believe they need an expert to complete. Sometimes, the team members can understand what's going on as pairs. Sometimes, two heads are better than one.
- Ask the team members to swarm on the work. This works especially well when the team members use test-driven development and generate automated tests first, so the tests support the team's work.

You may have to help the teams transition past specialist thinking.

15.3 The Teams Have Dependencies on Other Teams

Are your product development teams able to work through your entire stack to produce a feature?

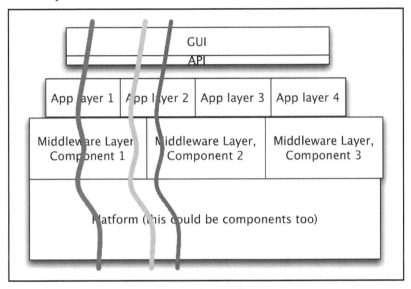

Figure 15.2: Implement by Feature

In the picture Implement by Feature, you can see how feature teams would implement an entire small feature through the stack. If a team doesn't have the right people to deliver a full feature, what impediments can you remove so the team does have all the people it requires on the team to implement a full feature?

Sometimes, teams have much more complex features because they have dependencies on other teams. I see this a lot with component teams. Each team is able to implement their part. However, no one can realize the value of a feature until all the component teams finish their pieces.

One team I coached explained that they had "curlicue" features (see Figure 15.3 on page 190). They didn't have straight-line features.

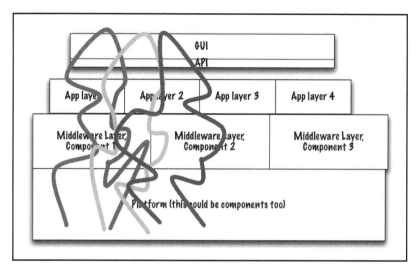

Figure 15.3: Curlicue Features

They had interdependencies with other teams that led to large features that looked like the image, Curlicue Features.

Sometimes, curlicue features might be an artifact of Conway's Law. Imagine that on your program, the middleware people are in Paris, the UI people are in Edinburgh, the App layer 1 people are in Denver, the App layer 2 people are in Raleigh, and the Platform people are in San Francisco. You need all those teams to deliver one feature. The features are large and have dependencies on other teams.

When you hear "dependencies on other teams" or experts, you know that The Teams Are Not Feature Teams (page 17). I've provided suggestions for helping the teams become feature teams. At the least, ask the teams to create kanban boards so everyone can visualize where the feature is in its development.

15.4 Your Features Span Several Iterations

What I see in some teams quite new to agile: Do your features span iterations? Are they too large to finish in a day or so?

If so, make your features smaller. Making features smaller will help the team see its progress. The smaller features also provide feedback to the product owner/customer. That feedback will help the product owner make the stories smaller and will help the team complete its work inside the iteration. If you are using kanban, this is similar to seeing a board not change for weeks while the same features are still on the board, nothing moving. You are also likely doing staged integration.

If you need help making stories smaller, try defining scenarios, instead of stories. Then, see if you can work by value in the scenario. See Jeff Patton's *User Story Mapping*, (PAT14), Gojko Adzic's, *Impact Mapping: Making a big impact with software products and projects*, (ADZ12), and Adzic and Evans' *Fifty Quick Ideas to Improve Your User Stories*, (ADZ14). Review Pawel Brodzinski's *Minimal Indispensable Feature Set*, (BRO14).

15.5 You Don't Have Frequent-Enough Deliverables

If you have frequent internal releases—regardless of whether or not you release your product—everyone can see the product grow.

If you don't have monthly deliverables, ask teams to release something complete each week. That will help them see their impediments to releasing monthly.

When everyone can see the product grow, everyone can gain feedback on the product's progress. The product owners learn about the stories—how valuable they are, how large or small they are, and how easy or difficult they are to implement. The developers and testers learn how well they do at developing and testing the product. The UX designers learn how well they do at user experience design for this product. And so on.

When you make your product releasable often, you practice.

Some of you are saying, "We release multiple times every day. I don't see what's so great about releasing once every single month." If you have a large program of more than 15 teams—especially a program with hardware—it can be quite difficult to release anything, never mind release a product of value once a month.

15.6 Teams Don't Finish When They Say They Are Done

Some teams, especially those new to agile or lean, have problems with the idea of "done." That's when you start hearing about "done-done" or "done-done-done."

The way to get to done is to use the technical practices: automated system testing, automated test-driven development (ATDD), test-driven development (TDD) or behavior-driven development (BDD), and especially continuous integration on small stories.

Some teams and product owners have a lot of trouble with the idea of small stories. Some teams have a ton of trouble integrating the technical practices, because they have not practiced them daily as part of their professional lives.

You, as a program manager, can't make teams change. You can invite them to change. You can ask for the results you want. You can support them and ask, "How can I help?"

Explain, "I don't care how many features you finish in an iteration or in flow. I care that the feature is done. Once you really get to done reliably, we can start thinking about increasing velocity, *if you want to*. However, in my experience, small features that are no longer than two days long will help you accomplish several things:

- Finishing your features when you say you will.
- Seeing your progress better.
- Getting to done when you are done, and not doing more than you need to, for a given feature.

15.6.1 Develop communities of practice to help teams as peers

If some teams have trouble with some practices, they need help with change. Remember, people change one person at a time. Try this checklist:

1. Do people know what they need to do? Maybe people need training first.
2. Do people have adequate tools to perform their jobs? Maybe people don't have the tools they need. If your program is anything like the programs I've seen, some teams do not have access to the same infrastructure as other teams. It's crazy, but true. Fix the infrastructure problem, and you have fixed the problem.
3. Explain the risks of non-compliance with the desired results. Some people and teams don't realize the effect their actions have on other people and teams.

Remember, on an agile program, the agile program manager facilitates the work of the projects/feature teams. The agile program manager does not demand. The agile program manager does not lay down the law. The agile program manager does not say, "Here's how it's going to be, folks."

On the other hand, the agile program manager can point out the consequences or risks of not taking certain actions. "If we don't integrate as we go, we will never meet this demonstration date." Or, the trade show date, or the desired release date, or some other date. Or, manage some other risk.

I'm quite happy to explain the risks to the feature teams. They are adults. But if the software program manager explains the risks, or even says, "I have a funny feeling about this, and I can't explain it, but I think this is risky, and I would like your help on managing the risk of not integrating as we proceed," most people will respond and say, "Okay, let's see how we can get closer to continuous integration." Or, they will say, "Hey, this is really hard," or "This is really expensive," or "We know how to do it with lots of branches which is crazy," or "We only know how to do it if we break the build" or any number of other problem statements.

They're not stupid. They may be intimidated by technical practices, but they are not stupid. And, they may have doubts about the cost of servers or breaking the builds—doubts which are real.

15.7 Principles of Troubleshooting Agile Team Issues

1. Help each team deliver as often as possible. The principle is: "Deliver working software frequently."
2. Invite teams to change. Don't mandate a change. Instead, create a vision of a better program with the changes. The principle is: "Build projects around motivated individuals. Trust them to get the job done."
3. If teams are not retrospecting to see what causes them to have trouble, ask them to do so. The principle is: "Reflect and adjust at regular intervals."

CHAPTER 16

Integrating Agile and Not-Agile Teams in Your Program

You might want to use agile or lean approaches on your programs. But, what if you have a mixture of agile and waterfall teams? Or, maybe you have component teams instead of feature teams. Maybe you have people who talk agile, but don't work in an agile way.

If you are in that position, here are some alternatives to help your program become more agile. You will have to decide how much external help you need from coaches or trainers. Do not expect that you can move an entire program—especially not a large one—to agile by yourself.

Agile and lean are based around trust, autonomy, and collaboration. You trust people to deliver unless they don't. If they don't, you can ask them what their obstacles are and if they need help removing them. Treating people like adults, and having adult expectations of them, gives you most of the same results as asking for the same stuff and calling it "agile."

People will live up to your expectations of them.

You can say, "Here are the results I want as the program manager. If you can work this way, we will get the benefits."

If the ideas here don't work, consider the ideas in What If Agile and Lean are Not Right for You (page 201). Agile and lean program management are supposed to make your life easier, not more difficult.

16.1 Waterfall Teams Are Part of Your Program

Some teams don't know or don't want to use agile approaches on their projects. And, they are on your program. You have possibilities for managing the interdependencies with the agile teams.

1. Make sure you use deliverable-based planning for all the projects. If your program uses the ideas in Create the Agile Roadmap (page 44), you will use deliverable-based planning.

2. Ask the non-agile projects to determine their deliverable-based milestones, preferably one each month. You can ask the non-agile projects to deliver their deliverables once each month.

3. Ask all projects to use an incremental approach to delivery. No waiting until the end of the program to deliver. For many people on the waterfall teams, this is a huge change. The developers might not want to release their code into the code base until it is "all done." The testers might not know how to test partially implemented features. And, if the testers on the non-agile projects are still testing a previous project or release, you will have to remove that multitasking obstacle. You need to work with the product owners for the non-agile teams, so they create an agile roadmap and short interim releases.

4. Use rolling wave planning to plan the program. You don't have to keep a four-week wave—you can use a shorter wave. Do not use a wave longer than four weeks. The program needs to release something each month.

5. Ask the waterfall teams to use kanban so they can see their WIP. You and they need to know if they have a ton of work in progress that they are not delivering.

6. Ask each project to measure their cumulative flow. Be ready to explain to the teams or project managers how to do this. Each team needs to see all their work in progress. This will help them all see their dependencies. The more interdependencies the teams have, the more they have to talk with each other to break them. They might need more deliverables. They might need a

kanban board to see bottlenecks across the program. You, the software program team, and the core team can help with these problems. But, until they see work in progress, they won't know what they need.

The non-agile projects will start to look like staged delivery or design-to-schedule life cycle projects. In a sense, that's cheating, because they are no longer strict waterfall projects. That will work. No one gets credit for strict adherence to waterfall or agile. People get credit for successful projects and programs.

If you do have people who audit your program for a strict adherence to any approach, that is a risk to your program. You can show good software practices with any approach, even using both agile and not agile in the same program. But, you don't need anyone looking over your shoulder.

If your not-agile projects have project managers, you may have to coach the project managers into working in new and different ways. You, the program manager, have to understand all about project management and servant leadership. Explain the results you want and when you need them. Treat the project managers as if they are adults. Help the project managers learn how to manage in a servant leadership way.

The not-agile project staff may feel as if you are "forcing" them to transition to agile. You are not. However, they may be unaccustomed to deliverable-based milestones. Invite People to Experiment (page 88) and measure their results.

You may need to provide training or a coach for these teams. Do not expect people with a controlling-project mindset to automatically adjust to an adaptable-project mindset.

16.2 You Have Teams that Produce Incrementally, But Not in an Agile Way

Some teams think they are agile if they use the words. These teams have large features that take at least a two-week iteration or longer to release. The teams work on features, so they are developing incrementally. However their increments are so large that they have tremendous work in progress, or that they take months to finish something before they receive any feedback. These teams cannot complete a feature in two or even three weeks.

Ask the product owners to create feature sets that the team can help break down into smaller features. Explain that you want the team to integrate something that looks like a feature into the code base every single day.

You may need to provide the team with some coaching or training. I have met many teams who have not even read one agile book and don't realize how to work in an agile or lean way.

16.3 You Have Teams that Prototype and Don't Complete Features

Some prototyping can be quite helpful. For example, in an architectural spike, the output might be a proof of concept or a prototype. However, if a team only prototypes and never finishes features, that is a problem.

Ask the team to create a kanban board so everyone can see the state of the features. Ask the team to define and manage their WIP. Ask the team to define what done means for them. Ask the team to conduct a retrospective so they understand what they did and how they did it.

Now, the team and you have data. Maybe the team can take it from here. Maybe the team needs help in some way and the kanban board will show everyone that data.

I worked with a team that had this problem. Their testers were multitasking on so many other projects I wondered how the team even had the feedback on their prototypes.

Another team didn't realize their definition of done was inadequate.

Teams who don't complete features need some sort of problem-solving advice. Don't impose help on the team until you have the data. Consider helping them learn how to discover their data for themselves.

16.4 Principles of Integrating Agile and Not-Agile Teams in Your Program

1. Use deliverable-based planning for the program and for each team. The more often each team has deliverables, the more they will see what they have to deliver to the program and when. With those deliverables, you will be able to see any team's obstacles. The principles are: "Eliminate waste" and "Working software is the primary measure of progress."

2. There are no prizes for "how agile any team is." The only thing that counts is delivering working product. The principles are: "Deliver early and often to satisfy the customer" and "Empower the team."

3. Only take fully-staffed teams and fully-assigned people on your program. Do not take multitasked people on your program. The principle is: "The best architectures, requirements, and designs emerge from self-organizing teams." If you have trouble with this principle, see Troubleshooting Agile Team Issues (page 179).

CHAPTER 17

What to Do If Agile and Lean Are Not Right for You

You've read this book, and you think, "Okay, this is great, but it's not going to work for me, our program, or our organization."

Maybe you've decided the culture won't support agile and lean now, or you have many waterfall projects in addition to some agile projects in your program. Maybe you're new to agile, your iterations are longer than two weeks, and your risk is too high. Maybe your managers want to exert too much control in the projects over what people do (move people like chess pieces), and not manage the project portfolio.

You have options. You do not have to run a program in waterfall. You can take advantage of everything you know about project management, about deliverable-based planning, about cross-functional collaborative teams, about reducing work in progress—everything you know *from* agile and lean and good project management practices to make your project successful.

This is called "thinking."

Your organization pays you, and anyone involved in a program, to think. Especially if you are the program manager and are supposed to manage risks and remove obstacles.

Some of the ideas in this chapter might work for you. I encourage you to try them. Along the way, as people relax and learn more about agile and lean approaches, maybe you can apply more ideas.

Don't call these ideas agile or lean. They're not. They are reasonable, practical, pragmatic approaches to completing programs.

See what might work for you. I encourage you to involve the people on your program. Whatever you do, don't call them "best practices." That will kill people's excitement about trying anything. If you need a name for these ideas, call them "potentially useful practices."

Invite people and teams to experiment, measure their progress, and reflect. If the data says things aren't working and you've given the idea enough time, try something else.

The worst thing that happens is you return to waterfall with no replanning. As we know, that is the worst thing that can happen. Because on a program, Murphy's Law is waiting to happen. Murphy will make you replan.

Here are some possibilities, depending on your program risks.

17.1 Try an Incremental Life Cycle

For many years, I used staged delivery as my preferred approach, and timeboxed everything, so we had a chance of making management's mandated dates.

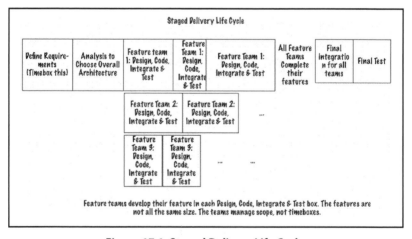

Figure 17.1: Staged Delivery Life Cycle

A staged delivery or design-to-schedule life cycle are *incremental* life cycles. These life cycles allow you to build features, one feature at

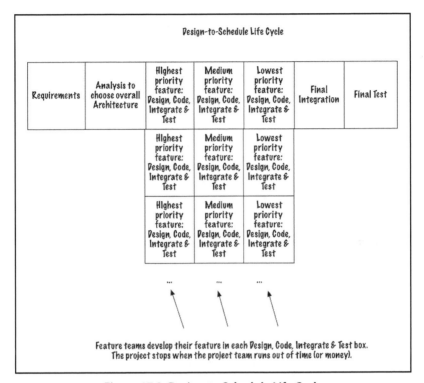

Figure 17.2: Design-to-Schedule Life Cycle

a time, integrating and testing as you proceed. For more information on incremental life cycles, see *Manage it! Your Guide to Modern, Pragmatic Project Management*, (ROT07).

Notice that not all of the features are the same size. The teams do not necessarily align on feature boundaries. Do not kid yourself. This could be difficult if your features are big, and you do not timebox the features. Your teams may not be able to integrate without the assistance of a release engineering or some sort of integration team if the features are not small.

I have used Staged Delivery to manage a program. I found timeboxing to be a big help. I timeboxed the initial requirements gathering to no more than one or two weeks. I explained to the product managers or anyone else involved, "Please provide a ranked list, as in 1, 2, 3, 4, down to 57 or 98 or whatever by two weeks from now. You can change it later. But we need to start on the most important features. The most important features will drive our architectural decisions." We did not descend into "requirements hell."

I also timeboxed the BDUF (Big Design Up Front) piece. All of my experience tells me that the initial architecture will be wrong. I much prefer it when we do three features first and then select an architecture. However, I am not always successful convincing the architects of this. If you aren't successful either, timebox this effort to no more than two weeks.

If you already have many people on the program, make sure you have people working on learning how to work together. See How to Start a Program With More People Than You Need (page 161) and apply those principles to this approach.

Now, you can timebox the features. For example, you can say, "Let's make sure we can deliver something every month. Let's timebox all of our features to fit into a one-month timebox."

These life cycles are not agile approaches. They will not revolutionize your culture in the same way as agile does. However, if you cannot move to two-week iterations, and complete features every day or so in your feature teams, try these approaches.

Principles I use in an incremental life cycle:

1. Timebox everything. You don't have to work in iterations, but make sure you timebox features.
2. Use monthly milestones and integrate everything at least every month. More often is better.
3. Make sure you have a *product* release or a demonstration at least every once a quarter. Every month is better. Why? So you can see the product.

This is incremental work, not iterative and incremental. However, you will see the product grow, month by month, especially if you use two-week or one-month timeboxes.

17.2 Organize by Feature Team

Instead of organizing by architectural component, consider organizing by feature team. You don't have to change where people sit. That might be too much change. But do change their allegiance, from their function, to their feature set.

Make no mistake, this has the potential to manifest enormous change in the organization.

I introduce this in this way: "I am going to be asking for monthly, visible deliverables by *feature*. The best way I know how to accomplish that is for people to work together in feature teams. I realize I am asking you to split up the developer, tester, writer, business analyst, and all the other teams that sit together. It's okay if you groan now. I have seen cross-functional teams that create features work together really well.

"In addition, to make sure you folks still know who you are, and know the issues that are difficult for you, I'd like to see you have "Community of Practice" meetings every week or every other week. These are learning sessions, or knowledge sharing sessions. These are for your professional development.

"I realize this is a big change. How about if we experiment, and try it for a month and see what happens?"

When you frame things as an experiment, you invite people to try it. You are not mandating any change. You are asking them to try something. Make sure you schedule a retrospective to see what works and doesn't work at the end of the month. Include the retrospective on the schedule when you ask for this reorganization.

17.3 Learn to Release Interim Deliverables

Before I learned about agile, I had a guideline that the entire program had to deliver something every month. That is, we, as a program, had to see something visible every month. Believe me, this was a struggle with hardware. We often had to see a simulation.

The best thing you can do for your program is to learn to deliver often. Why? You build trust between the feature teams by delivering to each other. You build trust between the program and your management team by delivering. Delivering is crucial.

If you say to the technical teams on the program, "We might not be ready for agile. But there's this idea in agile that I think we can do: Monthly deliverables. Do you think we can have every team deliver something every month?"

Now, sit back and listen to people. Sometimes, when you say things such as, "We might not be ready..." people take it as a challenge. "Yes we are," they say. Other people agree with you.

You can always say, "Here are the principles that we want to live by;" and then suggest that releasing early and often is one of the principles.

17.4 Learn How to Reduce Batch Size With a Large Program

Back in Create the Big Picture Roadmap (page 47), I explained the differences between epics, themes, and feature sets. If you have large features on your program, it's often because the product owners do not know how to break apart the feature sets into small, one- or two-day features.

The teams may have to help their product owners break the epics, themes, and feature sets into small stories. The product owners may not have the product expertise to know how to do so.

If the product owners don't have the time to break apart the epics, themes, or feature sets into small stories, you have a major risk and an impediment to your program. What else are these people doing? I am sure they are not twiddling their thumbs. I suspect they are not working full time on your program. You can fix that.

The smaller the batch size—the story—the faster the teams will work. The faster they work, the faster they will integrate, maintaining momentum on your program. Help the product owners reduce batch size. The product roadmap and backlog creation is key to your program's success.

17.5 Try Release Trains

If you are not ready for agile, you can use release trains, and see your product grow with each release.

The teams might work in mini-waterfalls instead of by feature. The value of a release train is that you have to release something every train.

When you use release trains externally, you commit to yourself and to your customers to release your product on a particular date every quarter. The quarter is the iteration. If you are a program manager, you can ask your teams to consider an iteration of somewhere between six weeks and eight weeks. At worse, you can ask your teams to commit to an iteration of 12 weeks.

In a program, you are not an external customer—you are internal. Because you are working with project teams—feature teams—you don't need marketing collateral or training to be ready internally; you only need the software to be integrated and possibly to be married to the hardware. That is difficult enough—you want the non-agile project teams to start learning how to use deliverable-based planning in small chunks, and to focus on what the customer will be able to use.

The release train is not agile, because it takes too long to obtain feedback from a product owner or a customer. However, release trains allow you to manage risk. These teams will likely be using small waterfalls, unless you can convince them to use iterative or incremental life cycles. But you as a program manager can manage the program risk better with the train because it allows you to obtain those small deliverables periodically. Sure, the deliverables aren't every two weeks; they probably aren't every four weeks, either. But they are more often than every six months, and that's an improvement.

Release trains decouple the releasing of the product from the projects. That is, release trains set their dates in stone in advance, and are often tied to a specific date in the quarter or the month, like a train's timetable. Then the contents of the train are determined by what the teams think they can accomplish. When a feature is done, it is eligible to be released. Release trains never extend the timebox, just as trains never change the time they leave the station.

This is what a release train looks like:

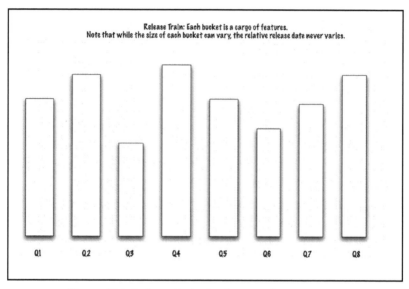

Figure 17.3: Release Train: Each train releases on the same relative day each quarter

I am using quarters here because the picture looks better; you could use months as an alternative. You can use any periodic iteration, such as six weeks or eight weeks—as long as you use a consistent iteration. The iterations build a cadence for your program.

Between releases, you can ask the teams to organize so they build by feature. Often, teams use an incremental life cycle such as design-to-schedule or a staged delivery life cycle because they fit the parameters of the release train so well. Some teams who are comfortable with Rational Unified Process (RUP) use that.

You could use a kanban board to limit work in progress and still make sure features get to done. Remember, it doesn't matter what life cycle the team uses; it only matters that you have finished features in the codebase by the end of the iteration, when the train is ready to pull away from the station.

A release train does not have the same focus and urgency a shorter timebox has. When your timebox is eight or 12 weeks, other problems can arise and change the backlog for the timebox. Remember, the project team only gets feedback once their train leaves the station.

In programs, committing to a ranked backlog for a train can be tricky. Why? Because the product owner will want to change the roadmap more frequently than once a quarter. Changing the roadmap can prevent the teams from completing anything.

I recommend you use kanban for the non-agile team. The team takes take work off the queue, always working on the most important feature. Since they are working in a timebox, does it matter which features they work on? No.

Release trains provide you more predictability. They reduce risk, compared to a waterfall. They do not provide the ability to change often.

Measure your time to a releasable deliverable, as in Measure the Time to Your Releasable Deliverable. Make sure your time to release stays at whatever cadence you decide, and that it doesn't increase because you need hardening sprints.

And what about those of you who have long lead-time items, such as hardware of some variety or mechanical engineering parts? Use deliverable-based planning and rolling-wave scheduling, and keep those parts of the program using release trains for their design.

Managing a program of agile and non-agile projects is a fact of program management life; it's not going to go away. You will need all the tips and tricks to make it easy. Release trains are an old technique, but you can apply them in a new way. What have you got to lose?

17.6 Principles for What to Do if Agile and Lean Are Not Right for You

If agile and lean are not going to work in your organization, keep these principles in mind:

1. Work by feature, whenever possible. Make those features small, so the teams can integrate them continuously. The principle is: "Deliver early and often to satisfy the customer."

2. Tell the teams you want them to work in small-world networks, to be autonomous, collaborative, and exploratory. Just because you're not doing agile or lean does not mean you can't ask people to work in a highly collaborative way. Do so. The principles are: "Empower the team" and "The best architectures, requirements, and designs emerge from self-organizing teams."

3. Maintain your stance as a servant leader. Keep your focus on problem-solving and obstacle removal for the feature teams. You can still run the program teams as if they are agile or lean teams, solving problems across the organization. The principle is: "Business people and developers must work together."

Annotated Bibliography

[ADZ12] Adzic, Gojko. *Impact Mapping: Making a big impact with software products and projects*. Provoking Thoughts, 2012. Understand what you want to build.

[ADZ14] Adzic, Gojko and David Evans. *Fifty Quick Ideas to Improve Your User Stories*. Neuri Consulting LLP, 2014. Many teams struggle with user stories. This little book can help you improve what you plan to deliver.

[AMA11] Amabile, Teresa and Steven Kramer. *The Progress Principle: Using Small Wins to Ignite Joy, Engagement, and Creativity at Work*. Harvard Business Review Press, Boston, 2011. They have completed the research that says we like to finish work in small chunks so we can make progress.

[BEL06] Belshee, Arlo. *Promiscuous Pairing and Beginner's Mind: Embrace Inexperience*. IEEE Computer Society, 2005. We often think pairing has to be between similar experienced people. Not true.

[BRO14] Brodzinski, Pawel. *Minimal Indispensable Feature Set* at http://brodzinski.com/2014/12/minimal-indispensable-feature-set.html, 2014. What do you really need to build? How little can that be?

[BRO95] Brooks, Frederick P. *The Mythical Man-Month: Essays on Software Engineering, Anniversary Edition (2nd Edition)* Addison-Wesley, Boston, 1995. Learn from a master.

[DER06] Derby, Esther and Diana Larsen. *Agile Retrospectives: Making Good Teams Great.* Pragmatic Bookshelf, Dallas, TX and Raleigh, NC, 2006. The classic work about retrospectives.

[DWE07] Dweck, Carol. *Mindset: The New Psychology of Success.* Ballantine Books, New York, 2007. This book discusses the fixed mindset and the growth mindset. If you have the fixed mindset, you believe you can only do what you were born with. If you have the growth mindset, you believe you can acquire new skills and learn. The growth mindset allows you to improve, a little at a time.

[EDM12] Edmondson, Amy C. *Teaming: How Organizations Learn, Innovate, and Compete in the Knowledge Economy.* Jossey-Bass, San Francisco, 2012. How self-organized teams really work, and what we need to make them work in different cultures.

[FOW03] Fowler, Martin. *Who Needs an Architect?*, IEEE Software July-August 2003, pp 2-4, also at http://martinfowler.com/ieeeSoftware/whoNeedsArchitect.pdf. Read this if you want to understand what architects can do for you, and what they should not do. Wonderful article about the value of architecture.

[GLI15] Gonçalves, Luis and Ben Linders. *Getting Value out of Agile Retrospectives: A Toolbox of Retrospective Exercises.* Leanpub, 2015. More retrospective exercises for your consideration.

[GRE02] Greenleaf, Robert K. *Servant Leadership: A Journey into the Nature of Legitimate Power and Greatness, 25th Anniversary Edition.* Paulist Press, New York, 2002. The original and definitive text on servant leadership. The forewords and afterwords provide significant value to understanding how servant leaders work.

[HAC02] Hackman, J. Richard. *Leading Teams: Setting the Stage for Great Performances.* Harvard Business Review Press, Boston, 2002. The classic work about what a team is, including what a self-managing or self-organizing team is.

[HAM14] Hammarberg, Marcus and Joakim Sundén. *Kanban in Action.* Manning, Shelter Island, NY, 2014. Terrific introduction to kanban.

[KEI08] Keith, Kent M. *The Case for Servant Leadership.* Greenleaf Center for Servant Leadership, Westfield, IN, 2008. Useful because it's short, sweet, and specific.

[MOA13] Modig, Niklas and Pär Åhlström. *This is Lean: Resolving the Efficiency Paradox.* Rheologica Publishing, 2013. Possibly the best book about how managers should consider agile and lean. A wonderful discussion of resource efficiency vs. flow efficiency.

[PAT14] Patton, Jeff. *User Story Mapping: Discover the Whole Story, Build the Right Product.* O'Reilly, Sebastopol, CA, 2014. A terrific way to explain your stories to yourself. This book will help you move from epics and themes to stories your feature teams can build.

[POP03] Poppendieck, Mary and Tom Poppendieck. *Lean Software Development: An Agile Toolkit.* Addison-Wesley, Boston, 2003. The first book to provide a lean approach to software.

[REI09] Reinertsen, Donald G. *The Principles of Product Development Flow: Second Generation Lean Product Development.* Celeritas Publishing, Redondo Beach, CA, 2009. A classic for understanding batch size and weighted shortest job first.

[BCD05] Rothman, Johanna and Esther Derby. *Behind Closed Doors: Secrets of Great Management.* Pragmatic Bookshelf, Dallas, TX and Raleigh, NC, 2005. We describe the Rule of Three and many other management approaches and techniques in here.

[ROT07] Rothman, Johanna. *Manage It! Your Guide to Modern, Pragmatic Project Management.* Pragmatic Bookshelf, Dallas, TX and Raleigh, NC, 2007. If you want to know more about how to estimate task size, establish a project rhythm, or see a project dashboard, this is the book for you. I have references about why multitasking is crazy in here.

[ROT09] Rothman, Johanna. *Manage Your Project Portfolio: Increase Your Capacity and Finish More Projects.* Pragmatic Bookshelf, Dallas, TX and Raleigh, NC, 2009. Sometimes, program managers encounter project portfolio decisions with the feature set, or the request for people to multitask. This book helps you manage all the work in your project portfolio. I also have more references about why multitasking is crazy in here.

[RE14] Rothman, Johanna and Jutta Eckstein. *Diving for Hidden Treasures: Finding The Real Value in Your Project Portfolio.* Practical Ink, 2014. A book about Cost of Delay and how to see how those costs affect your project portfolio.

[ROT15] Rothman, Johanna. *Predicting the Unpredictable: Pragmatic Approaches to Estimating Project Schedule or Cost.* Practical Ink, 2015. What you need to know about estimation and what to do when your estimate is wrong.

[SHI08] Shirky, Clay. *Here Comes Everybody: The Power of Organizing with Organizations.* Penguin Books, New York, 2008. Why collaboration works, even when people don't know each other. It's fascinating. Where I first learned the term "small-world networks."

[SIN09] Singer, David J., PhD., Captain Norbert Doerry, PhD., and Michael E. Buckley. *What is Set-Based Design?* at http://www.doerry.org/norbert/papers/SBDFinal.pdf, 2009. A readable paper about what set-based design is and how to use it.

[SNB07] Snowden, David J. and Mary E. Boone. *A Leader's Framework for Decision Making* in *Harvard Business Review*, November 2007. The introductory article about the Cynefin Framework.

[SH06] Subramaniam, Venkat and Andy Hunt. *Practices of an Agile Developer: Working in the Real World.* Pragmatic Bookshelf, Dallas, TX and Raleigh, NC, 2006. I first learned about the term "PowerPoint architects" from Venkat and Andy. I'd seen those kinds of architects, of course. If you want to become an agile developer, or an agile architect, start here.

[TIK14] Tikka, Ari. *Coordination Chaos* at http://www.slideshare.net/aritikka/coordination-chaos-41883070, 2014. Learn how experts can make life much more complicated.

[WIR11] Wirfs-Brock, Rebecca. *Starting with Landing Zones* at http://wirfs-brock.com/blog/2011/07/20/introducing-landing-zones/, 2011. How to trade off architectural qualities on the way to done.

[SHU14] Unknown. *Secret to Shutterstock Tech Teams* at http://bits.shutterstock.com/2014/05/08/the-secret-to-shutterstock-tech-teams/ What a real manager does with real teams.

Glossary

If you are not familiar with the terms I've used, here are the definitions.

Adaptive: Any approach that allows you to adjust your practices or behavior to the current reality.

Agile: You work in small chunks, finishing work that is valuable to the customer in the order the customer specifies. The value of working in an agile way is that you have the ability to change quickly, because you complete work.

Backlog: Ranked list of items that need to be completed for the product.

Cost of Delay: The revenue impact you incur when you delay a project. Aside from "missing" a desired release date, you can incur Cost of Delay with multitasking, or waiting for experts, or from one team waiting for another in the program. All of these problems—and more—lead to delay of your product release.

Community of Practice: A way to share knowledge among people who belong to different teams, and share the same interests or function. For example, in a program, you might have an architecture community of practice that helps any developer learn how to evolve the design of the product. A test community of practice would provide a forum for testers to discuss what and how to test.

Flow: The team takes a limited number of items to complete, and uses the WIP limit instead of a timebox as a way to control how much work the team takes.

Generalizing Specialist: Someone who has one skill in depth, and is flexible enough to be able to work across the team to help move a feature to done.

Hardening Sprint: If a team does not complete all the work they need for a release, they may need a hardening sprint to complete all the testing for a release. This is an indication the teams are not really getting to done each iteration. They have work in progress past the end of the iteration.

Inch-pebble: Inch-pebbles are one-to-two day tasks that are either done or not done.

Iteration: A specific timebox. For agile projects, that time is normally one to four weeks. In programs, I like even smaller iterations because you want feedback more often and want to build momentum.

Kanban: Literally the Japanese word for "signboard." A scheduling system for limiting the amount of work in progress at any one time.

Lean: A pull approach to managing work that looks for waste in the system.

MVP: Minimum viable product. What is the minimum you can do, to create an acceptable product? This is not barely good enough quality. This is shippable product. However, this is minimal in terms of features.

Pairing: When two people work together on one task.

Parking Lot: This is a place to put issues you don't want to lose but don't necessarily want to address at this time.

Spike: If you cannot estimate a story, timebox some amount of work (preferably with the entire team) to learn about it. Then you will be able to know what to do after the day or two timebox.

Servant Leadership: An approach to managing and leading where the leader creates an environment in which people can do their best work.

The leader doesn't control the work; the team does. The leader trusts the team to provide the desired results.

Sprint: An iteration in Scrum.

Swarming: When the team works together to move a feature to done, all together.

Technical Debt: Shortcuts a team takes to meet a deliverable. Teams might incur technical debt on purpose, as a tactical decision. Technical teams can have architectural, design, coding, and/or testing debt. Program teams might have risk or decision debt—the insufficiency of work for managing risks or making decisions.

Timebox: A specific amount of time in which the person will attempt to accomplish a specific task.

WIP or Work in Progress: Any work that is not complete. When you think in lean terms, it is waste in the system. Note that you do not get credit for partially completed work in agile.

More from Johanna

I consult, speak, and train about all aspects of managing product development. I provide frank advice for your tough problems. I'm more interested in helping you become more effective than I am in sticking with some specific approach. There's a reason my newsletter is called the "Pragmatic Manager"—that's because I am!

If you liked this book, you might also like the other books I've written:

Diving for Hidden Treasures: Finding The Real Value in Your Project Portfolio[1]

Predicting the Unpredictable: Pragmatic Approaches to Estimating Project Schedule or Cost[2]

Project Portfolio Tips: Twelve Ideas for Focusing on the Work You Need to Start & Finish[3]

Manage Your Job Search[4]

Hiring Geeks That Fit[5]

Manage Your Project Portfolio: Increase Your Capacity and Finish More Projects[6]

---

[1] http://bit.do/ppvalue

[2] http://bit.do/predicting

[3] http://bit.ly/12porttips

[4] http://bit.do/myjs

[5] http://bit.do/hgtf

[6] http://bit.do/mypp

Manage It!: Your Guide to Modern, Pragmatic Project Management[7]

Behind Closed Doors: Secrets of Great Management[8]

In addition, I have essays in:

Readings for Problem-Solving Leadership[9]

Center Enter Turn Sustain: Essays on Change Artistry[10]

I'd like to stay in touch with you. If you don't already subscribe, please sign up for my email newsletter, the Pragmatic Manager,[11] on my website. Please do invite me to connect with you on LinkedIn,[12] or follow me on Twitter, @johannarothman.

I would love to know what you think of this book. If you write a review of it somewhere, please let me know. Thanks!

—Johanna

---

[7] http://bit.do/manageit

[8] http://bit.do/BCD

[9] https://leanpub.com/pslreader

[10] https://leanpub.com/changeartistry

[11] http://www.jrothman.com/pragmaticmanager/

[12] http://www.linkedin.com/in/johannarothman

Index

Made in the USA
San Bernardino, CA
10 August 2016